# LIFE OF

"I PROPOSE TO FIGHT IT OUT ON THIS LINE IF IT TAKES ALL SUMMER."

# U. S. GRANT.

S. WALKER & CO.

BOSTON

# LIFE

OF

# ULYSSES S. GRANT:

*HIS BOYHOOD, CAMPAIGNS, AND SERVICES, MILITARY AND CIVIL.*

BY

WILLIAM A. CRAFTS,

AUTHOR OF "A HISTORY OF THE SOUTHERN REBELLION."

With a Fine Portrait on Steel.

BOSTON:
SAMUEL WALKER AND COMPANY.
1868.

Stereotyped at the Boston Stereotype Foundry,

No. 19 Spring Lane.

U. S. Grant

# PREFACE.

---

The events related in the following Life of General Grant have been derived from authentic sources; and it has been the writer's aim to give a plain and truthful narrative, — like the subject himself, — without resorting to invention, high coloring, or rhetorical exaggeration, to add to the interest which attaches to one who occupies so eminent a position. It has also been the writer's purpose, avoiding minute details, controversy, and lengthy extracts from official reports, to offer a sufficiently brief and a popular Life of Grant, to meet the wants of numerous readers throughout the country who do not desire the larger and more costly works.

To the American people, who during the war were loyal to the Union, and since the war have been loyal to Liberty, Equality, and Justice, this little volume is committed, in the hope that under the administration of him whose career thus far is here sketched, they may see their country restored to peace and prosperity, with an enduring Union and universal liberty.

# CONTENTS.

## CHAPTER VII.



## CHAPTER VIII.



## CHAPTER IX.



## CHAPTER X.



## CHAPTER XI.

# LIFE

## OF

# GENERAL U. S. GRANT.

---

## CHAPTER I.

Ancestry. — Removal of his Grandfather to Ohio. — Parents and Birth. — At School and at Home. — Characteristics of his Boyhood. — Love of Horses. — Skill in managing them. — Too much for vicious Ponies. — Persistency. — The Load of Logs. — Prefers being a Soldier to being a Tanner. — Appointed a Cadet at West Point. — His Name. — U. S., "Uncle-Sam," and "Unconditional Surrender." — Career at West Point. — Solid Acquirements and medium Rank. — Brilliant Scholars not the ablest Generals. — Too plucky to be imposed upon. — Respects himself, and compels the Respect of others. — Patriotism. — Graduates at West Point.

THE ancestors of General ULYSSES S. GRANT came from Scotland, and probably belonged to the Scottish clan named Grant, whose ancient motto was, "Stand fast, stand firm, stand sure." The clan has never afforded a better illustration of that motto than the distinguished subject of this sketch. They first settled in Connecticut, from which state General Grant's grandfather, who was a soldier through the whole war of the revolution, removed to Westmoreland County, in Pennsylvania, and was a thrifty farmer there. About the year 1799, however, he emigrated with his family to what was then the North-western Territory, and became one of the pioneer settlers of Ohio, to the rich but wild lands of which the tide of emigration from the older states was then beginning to set. At the time of this removal Jesse R. Grant, the general's father, was a boy, who grew to manhood under the genial influences of that magnificent country, and the inuring difficulties of pioneer life. He added to the occupation of a farmer that of a tanner, and settling at Point Pleasant, in the County of Clermont, married Hannah Simpson, the daughter of another pioneer settler, also from Pennsylvania. He had learned his trade of tanner in Kentucky, but his aversion to slavery led him to settle in Ohio.

Hiram Ulysses Grant, now known to the world as General Ulysses S. Grant, was the eldest of six children, and was born on the 27th of April, 1822. His parents were quiet and unpretending, but persevering and thrifty, possessed of good sense, and governed by good principles. Grant felt their influence for good through all his early life; and his successful career is due, in no small degree, not only to his inherited temperament, but to his early training, and the influences of his home in the formation of his character. It was a humble home in which labor was necessary, but in which, also, the dignity of labor was justly appreciated and adorned with many virtues. In it Grant acquired habits of industry and fidelity to all his duties, of self-reliance, perseverance, and straightforward honesty. The influence of his mother, who was a woman of genuine strength of character, was very great, and was always well directed in moulding the elements of his character for future usefulness.

The early settlers of Ohio, especially those from New England and New York, carried with them a just appreciation of the advantages of education, and made provision for common schools. At one of these young Grant received such education as was then afforded. He was not a brilliant scholar, but he was faithful and persevering, and by dint of application and encouragement at home he mastered all the lessons required of him more successfully, and to better purpose, than boys of quicker and more showy abilities. He exhibited at school, and in all his youthful life, those qualities of faithfulness, patience, and perseverance, and a persistency in doing what was to be done, which have characterized him in after life, and have given him that success which has made him famous. In lessons he accomplished with credit all that was required of him, especially in mathematics, and at least acquired so much as enabled him, when appointed a cadet at West Point, to pass an examination as successfully as many who had enjoyed superior advantages, or were endowed with more brilliant mental qualities.

Nor was he idle at home. Like most boys in a similar condition of life, he had many duties to perform about his father's house and tannery; and to these duties, even if they were not always agreeable, he was always faithful. He was not afraid to work, or to lend a helping hand when anything was necessary to be done, and was especially apt at driving team or taking charge of horses. His work done, he applied himself to his lessons, receiving generous encouragement from his parents, and such assistance as they could render. He learned much by experience and observation, and acquired the habit of making practical application of what he learned by study. Thus his education at school and at home laid the foundation for the accomplishment of great deeds in his manhood, when his country imposed upon him the necessity.

When men have become famous, it is quite usual to find recorded numerous anecdotes of their sayings and doings in boyhood, which are characteristic of the qualities they exhibited in maturer years. If these are not readily found in family traditions or neighborly gossip, they are sometimes invented, or enlarged from some trivial occurrence which the subsequent fame of the subject alone would cause to be remembered. It is not proposed to repeat or to create any such myths concerning the boyhood of Grant. Doubtless many things occurred to him, and he did many things, which might, if duly recorded, add interest to his biography. But such things occur to all boys, and most of them do something characteristic, only there are but few whose after career renders it worth while to remember or enlarge upon such things to point a moral or adorn a biography.

But Grant's boyhood was not very remakable, and gave no special promise of future greatness, though a phrenologist once said *he would be President of the United States.* He was a downright, earnest, honest boy, quiet and unassuming, with indications of reserved power to meet emergencies. He was no boaster, but he exhibited self-reliance, persistency, and courage which could not but win the respect of his associates.

He was generous and good-natured, but his firmness did not allow him to be imposed upon. He was not disposed to quarrel or to fight on his own account, but it is related of him that he once fought and punished a Canadian boy who insulted the memory of Washington. He was not without ambition, but it was by no means the only motive of his actions, or led him to do more than faithfully and persistently attend to the duty in hand. He was patriotic, and had a laudable desire to serve his country as a soldier rather than as a politician. Though exhibiting no special aptitude for military life, except firmness and fidelity to duty, his modesty and reticence saw no attractions in the political field.

One of the traits of his character earliest to be developed was his love for horses, and his faculty of managing them. From his infancy he loved a horse, and learned to ride one long before he learned to read. When only seven and a half years old, during his father's absence, he harnessed to a sled a three-year-old colt, which had never been broken except to the saddle, and drove the animal all day, carrying loads of brushwood. He was afraid of no horse, and not only became an expert driver, but an excellent tamer and trainer of horses even before he was twelve years old. He taught them to pace with remarkable facility, and his neighbors, near and far, were very desirous of having his service in this line, though he was not inclined to become a mere horse-trainer. He rode with more than the skill of a circus-rider, for his rides were in the rough and open fields without the advantages of the "ring;" but his feats were for his own amusement and his own satisfaction, and not for the eye of any one else. He once or twice balked a tricky showman by safely riding a mischievous pony which was trained to throw all venturesome boys who mounted it, but was completely mastered by young Grant.

He not only loved a horse and knew how to tame, ride, and train him, but he early learned to know the points of a good horse, so that he could, even at twelve years old, judge of the quality and value of one. This love for and power over a horse, manifested, as in young Grant's case, in useful and practical ways, show both a genial side to his nature and a power to dare and to command.

His love of a good horse now is well known, and it is one of the homebred affections of his boyhood, which, with homebred habits and virtues, have adhered to him through all his life. He can "talk horse" with anybody, and has often evaded the questions of too inquisitive visitors, or concealed his plans and purposes, by a ready resort to that fruitful topic of conversation.

Another of his traits, which was early developed, was his perseverance, which was shown not only in his mastery of horses while yet a mere child, but was abundantly illustrated by labors which would have discouraged almost any boy of his age. When but twelve years old, and small for his age, he gave a remarkable example of practical application of his observation and of patient and persistent labor. He had gone to the woods expecting to find the men cutting timber and ready to load; but they were not there, and the young teamster had no idea of returning with an empty wagon if he could help it, though it required several men to lift the huge logs he was to carry. He looked around, and seeing a felled tree which lay with the trunk elevated at one end at a moderate angle with the ground, he at once thought of an expedient, and with self-reliance and perseverance set himself to work to put it in practice. With one of his horses he drew up the slope of the felled tree one end of a log he proposed to carry, and that being properly placed high enough for him to back the wagon under it, he in the same way drew, one at a time, two or three others, which made a load. That done, and the wagon being placed under the elevated ends, with his horse and chains he drew each log into it, and, securing his load, went quietly home, doubtless well pleased with his work, though making not the slightest boast.

His father could hardly believe the boy's assertion that he and the horse loaded the wagon; but he knew that Ulysses was never guilty of falsehood, and he soon had the work explained so that he was satisfied of its truth, though he still could not but wonder at his son's achievement. Such practical knowledge and persistent labor he exhibited all through his boyhood, and they furnish the key to some of the great successes of his after career.

That Grant was a boy of capacity and character, is proved by the fact that, without any special political or family influence, he received the appointment of cadet in the National Military Academy at West Point. He preferred being a soldier to being a tanner, and the country now knows that he chose wisely. He was nominated for admission to the Academy in 1839, by Hon. T. L. Hamer, member of Congress from the district in which he resided. By some mistake Mr.

Hamer gave his name as Ulysses S. Grant, probably confounding his name with that of a brother who bore the name of Simpson, his mother's maiden name. Grant applied to the authorities at West Point, and subsequently to the secretary of war, to have the error corrected, but those parties apparently did not think the matter of sufficient importance to demand their attention; or possibly they thought that the initials U. S. were very appropriate for a cadet educated at the expense of the United States, and destined to be an officer in the army of the United States. At any rate, the request was not complied with, and it was fated that Hiram Ulysses Grant was henceforth to be known as Ulysses S. Grant.

These initials were highly popular with the cadets, who soon gave Grant the nickname of "Uncle Sam," which he always retained in the army among the associates of his youth. They have proved popular with the people, too, who have delighted to associate with his the abbreviation of the national name, which he did so much to preserve. His first great victory, when he dictated terms to the rebels, gave other popular names to his initials, and he was enthusiastically hailed as "UNCONDITIONAL SURRENDER" GRANT. The name which a blunder assigned to him has thus become so identified with the history of the country, and with the love and admiration of the people, that neither he nor they could change it, or would desire to if they could.

At West Point, as at school, young Grant was not a brilliant scholar; but he was diligent in his studies, and by his persistency overcame all difficulties, and thoroughly mastered what it was necessary to learn. He was faithful to all his duties, and to the details of military life, though by no means placing too high an estimate upon the strict observance of such matters. His ambition was to perform his duties, and to acquire the knowledge for which he was sent to the Academy, and not to make a show either as a brilliant scholar or a punctilious martinet.

His characteristic persistency was illustrated at West Point not only by his application to studies, but by his playing the game of chess, of which he was fond. When he found a player who was at first more than a match for him, he persisted in playing till he "tired out" his antagonist, and at last beat him.

During the war of the rebellion West Point has abundantly proved that the most brilliant scholars do not make the ablest generals, and that great attainments in science, though they may produce skilful engineers, do not always lead to successful operations in the field, either in the way of strategy or the handling of troops. At the same time it has proved that the knowledge and training acquired there are not to be depreciated, but afford the surest basis for military success, and that those who attain only to a medium rank as cadets, if they profit by what they learn, may in war achieve great things for the country, and earn a wider and more enduring fame than that of brilliant scholars or accomplished engineers. Before the war, and for a long time after it commenced, old army officers and boards of examiners could not comprehend this; and it was vainly imagined that high scholars must make brilliant generals, and that able engineers would crush the rebellion. But stubborn facts and hard experience have shown the folly of such conclusions; and among those stubborn facts are the failure of George B. McClellan, the first scholar, and the signal success of Ulysses S. Grant, who ranked even below the middle of his class.

Grant's genial though retiring disposition, and quiet and unassuming manners, gradually made him many friends among the cadets; and when he became known, "Uncle Sam" was one of the most esteemed of his class, though not so popular, perhaps, as more talkative, rolicking, and demonstrative fellows. At first there were some who were disposed to make fun of the western country boy; and there were others, scions of southern aristocracy, who looked down upon him and his comparatively humble origin with contempt. He was one of the "mudsills" whom they despised. He proved, however, by his conduct, that he was worthy of respect even from these young aristocrats, and he taught those who made fun at his expense to cease their jokes. Though never disposed to quarrel, it is said that he found it necessary to maintain his own self-respect and dignity by punishing one or two who carried their jests too far. What was to be done in this line was, of course, done promptly and thoroughly, according to his manner of doing all things. Such rebukes were effectual; they established his pluck, and made him more generally respected and esteemed. His comrades found that he was not ashamed of his origin or any want of superficial polish; that he had no false pride which their jests could wound, but that he had a just self-respect; and this, coupled with his firmness and known perseverance, soon secured good conduct and respect towards him on their part.

Grant appreciated the advantages he enjoyed at West Point, and he was grateful to the country which afforded them. His youthful patriotism, too, received a new impulse from the associations with which he was surrounded, and the places celebrated in revolutionary history which lay all about him. Patriotism and duty to the country, which, as a cadet, he specially owed, were always acknowledged by him, and were the inspiring motives of his conduct in the day of the nation's peril. There were those with him there who never experienced such emotions; who daily saw the records of their country's heroes, and moved amid the scenes hallowed by the services and sacrifices of Washington and his compatriots, and yet never felt a throb of genuine patriotism, of love for the whole country, and never breathed a vow of fidelity to the government which educated them for its defence. Their pride was in their narrow states, and in the institution which made them rulers over an "inferior race." When the hour of the country's trial came, these men were found on the side of the rebellion, false to their country, false to their early associations, false to their oaths. If they have not gone down to traitors' graves, they may learn from the nobler career of Grant that patriotism and fidelity are their own great reward, and are gratefully acknowledged by a loyal people.

On the 1st of July, 1843, Grant, having passed the final examination at West Point, graduated the twenty-first scholar in his class, which numbered thirty-nine. It was not a high rank, but he had profited by what he had acquired there; and his natural characteristics of persistency and fidelity had been strengthened, so that he was better qualified for the duties of active service than many who possessed more showy attainments or a higher scientific knowledge. He was commissioned as brevet second lieutenant, and assigned to the Fourth Regiment of Infantry. His love of horses would probably have led him to select the cavalry arm of the service, but his comparative low rank as a scholar consigned him to the infantry.

## CHAPTER II.

In the Army. — Frontier Service. — Characteristics as a young Officer. — In Texas. — The Mexican War. — His first Battle. — Coolness and Bravery at Resaca de la Palma. — A steady, plucky Officer. — Appointed regimental Quartermaster. — Joins Scott's Army. — Tact, Energy, and Perseverance. — Not content with Quartermaster's Duties. — Participates in Battles. — Conspicuous Gallantry at Chepultepec. — Brevet First Lieutenant and Brevet Captain. — His Reputation earned by Merit and Service, not by Favoritism. — Return to the United States. — Married. — His Fortunes shared by his Wife; the higher Honors yet to be shared. — Ordered to the Pacific Coast. — Service in Oregon. — Promotion. — Resigns. — A Farmer in Missouri. — Careless Independence. — A Patriot, but no Politician. — Enters the Leather Business with his Father and Brother. — A higher Destiny reserved for him.

WHEN Grant received his first commission, the little army of the United States was occupied chiefly on the western frontier, a few troops only garrisoning the more important forts along the Atlantic seaboard, and on the shores of the Great Lakes. The Fourth Infantry was stationed on the western frontier to protect settlers from the Indians. The hostility of some of the Indians occasionally made the duties of the troops somewhat active, though no engagements occurred, and no very long marches were made. The duties of this service, however, were of no little advantage to the young officer, who was always ready to learn by experience, faithful to the details of his duty, and willing to work. Though the routine was tedious and irksome, nothing was neglected, and every opportunity of acquiring solid information upon matters connected with his profession was improved. As an officer he was the same good-natured and unassuming but firm, persevering, and reticent youth that he had been as a cadet at West Point. He was esteemed by his comrades and superiors as a young officer of moderate ability, but of undoubted pluck, perseverance, and self-reliance. In the ordinary duties of the army in time of peace, even on the frontier, he was not likely to become distinguished, nor to rise except by the slowest promotion. But those qualities for which he was justly esteemed were such as are needed in emergencies, and the value of which can be best proved by the inexorable demands of war.

In 1845, when the annexation of Texas threatened to involve the country in war with Mexico, the Fourth Infantry was sent to Texas, where it afterwards formed a part of General Taylor's "Army of Observation." Grant at this time was commissioned as full second lieutenant, and transferred to the Seventh Infantry; but at the request of the officers of the Fourth he was soon restored to that regiment. The advance of the Mexican army into Texas, where it besieged Fort Brown, precipitated the war with Mexico. General Taylor marched from Corpus Christi to the relief of the beleaguered fort, and encountered a large Mexican force on the march, when the battle of Palo Alto took place, May 8, 1846. Grant was with his regiment upon that field, and discharged his duties with a steadiness which was commended by his comrades and honorably mentioned by his superiors. The next day the more severe battle of Resaca de la Palma was fought, and the young lieutenant showed his quality as a soldier by his cool and persistent bravery. Those solid qualities, which in time of peace seemed to be of little account in a junior officer, began to reveal themselves and prove their value.

The Fourth Infantry remained with General Taylor till after the capture of Monterey, and participated in all the battles of old "Rough and Ready's" campaign, except that of Buena Vista. Grant's position as a cool and plucky officer was well established in his regiment, while his methodical attention to his duties were recognized by his superior officers, and led to his being placed upon the regimental staff as quartermaster. His regiment was among those detached from General Taylor's command, and sent to join the larger army under General Scott, which was to advance from Vera Cruz to the city of Mexico. His duties as regimental quartermaster, on a campaign like this into the heart of the enemy's country, were arduous and responsible, and required great tact, energy, and perseverance. They were discharged in a manner creditable to his administrative ability and his indomitable energy. But he was not satisfied with the faithful discharge of these most important duties; he desired to share in the dangers of the battle-field also, believing that "the post of danger is the post of duty." He participated in the bloody battles of Molino del Rey and Chepultepec, and was so conspicuous for his gallantry and successful service in the latter battle, where he bravely led a gallant charge, that he received honorable mention from General Worth, and was made brevet first lieutenant, and subsequently brevet captain, the latter commission dating from September 13, 1847, the date of the last-named battle.

Grant earned his reputation and his promotion in this Mexican campaign by his own solid abilities and actual achievements. He was unknown beyond his own regiment, was no pet at headquarters, and was not regarded by influential officers as a young man "of great promise" whom they desired to advance. Nor had he shown simply a temporary dash and enthusiasm, which at times are desirable on the battle-field, but are not always to be relied upon for good results. He was distinguished for cool and steady bravery, that inspired his men with confidence, and a persistency that overcame all obstacles. The substantial services which he rendered by these qualities were conspicuous to those about him, and were thus brought to the notice of superiors who had never heard of him. They were duly acknowledged by those superior officers, but nothing more than simple justice was done. It could not be said in his case that he received honorable mention or promotion either because he was a favorite with his superiors, or had made a brilliant display of bravery under the eye of the commanding general.

When the Mexican war was ended, and the victorious army returned to the United States, the Fourth Infantry was stationed at different posts on the northern frontier along the Great Lakes. While thus stationed, awaiting recruits to fill up the ranks thinned by death and discharges, the officers of the regiment enjoyed furloughs, after their long and arduous service. At this time Grant, still holding the rank of lieutenant, though a captain by brevet, married an accomplished and excellent lady, Miss Julia T. Dent, daughter of Frederick Dent, Esq., a merchant of St. Louis. Mrs. Grant has happily shared her husband's fortunes from the time when she married him, simply a lieutenant, till by his merits he has reached the highest military position ever given to an American officer; and it is to be hoped *that she will share with him those higher honors which the American people desire to bestow.*

In 1849 the Fourth Infantry was ordered to the Pacific, and a battalion to which Grant was attached was stationed in Oregon. While there he reached the rank of captain by regular promotion. In command of one of the posts of that region he faithfully discharged his duties, as in all his previous positions. But it was a time of profound peace, which promised to be of long duration, his duties were chiefly those of mere routine, promotion was slow, and active service of any kind was not likely to be required of him. He desired to provide more adequately for his wife and family, and under circumstances of less constraint to them. He therefore resigned his commission in 1854, the year following his promotion, and returned home to enter the pursuits of civil life.

He became the owner of a farm at Gravois, a few miles from St. Louis, and devoted himself to its cultivation. It was not altogether a new business for him, for in his boyhood he had learned much of the work of a western farm, and how to turn his hand to useful employment. He was not afraid to work himself, nor to lend a helping hand even to a black laborer. Quiet and unassuming still, he was not above his business,

2

and was quite as content to be called Farmer Grant as Captain Grant, though generally known by the latter title. He carried the produce of his farm to market himself, and might often have been seen driving his laden team through the streets of St. Louis or other river towns, and loading or unloading his wagon with a careless independence of all observers. He was reticent and modest, attended to his own affairs, and never troubled himself about those of other people, unless his advice or opinion was sought. He cared little for politics, and still less for parties, though he always felt the genuine patriotism which he had manifested by his service in the field. But with all his rough work, and his neglect of affairs which engross so much of the attention of men in this country, he did not forget his old studies, or the culture of his mind.

Thus he lived for some years, plodding on with characteristic perseverance in an occupation which, however honorable, was not always remunerative. But in 1860 he embraced the opportunity of entering what promised to be a more lucrative business, and engaged in the leather trade with his father and brother at Galena, Illinois. This was another business for which he was fitted by his early experience in his father's tannery, as he was also fitted for any business by his characteristic perseverance and fidelity to duties. He brought to it his usual quiet energy, and the plans of a well-disciplined mind, and was undoubtedly an acquisition to the firm. What he might have been in this new pursuit it is impossible to say, except that he probably would have been successful; for still, as when a boy, he knew no such word as fail. But it was reserved for him to show his real merit and ability on a wider and more important field, where his natural characteristics and his early training should have full force in the service of his country. Before he had a fair opportunity to show his business talent he was called to those higher duties.

## CHAPTER III.

The Rebellion. — Grant's Patriotism. — Raises a Company of Volunteers. — Tenders his Services to the Governor of Illinois. — Good Service. — Desires to take the Field. — Thinks of a Position on McClellan's Staff. — Fortunate Escape. — Appointed Colonel. — In Missouri. — Brigadier General. — An honorable Appointment. — At Cairo. — Kentucky Rebels. — Occupies Paducah. — Too prompt for Fremont. — Desires to advance against the Rebels. — Battle of Belmont. — Victory too much for new Troops. — Grant's Watchfulness. — "We have whipped them once, boys, and we can do it again." — Narrow Escape. — The Purpose accomplished. — Misrepresentations. — Grant's Generosity to his Subordinates. — "Better that I should suffer, than the Country lose the Services of such Officers." — Fort Henry. — Halleck's Want of Appreciation. — Fort Donelson. — Grant's Determination. — The Fort invested. — Engagements. — The rebel Prisoner. — Prompt Decision. — Attack and Victory. — Rebel Flag of Truce. — No Terms but *Unconditional Surrender*. — The Capture of Prisoners. — The Effect of the Victory on the Country.

GRANT, as before remarked, had never taken much interest in political affairs, both on account of his quiet, retiring disposition and his training as an officer, and he gave but little attention to the agitation which preceded secession and rebellion. But his patriotism led him to support the government against all assailants; and when the secessionists collected troops at Charleston, and planted batteries around Fort Sumter, he avowed himself without reserve for the government. When the war was opened by the attack on Sumter, and President Lincoln issued his proclamation calling for troops, he did not hesitate a moment where his duty lay.

The President's proclamation was issued on the 15th of April, 1861, and on the 19th Grant had raised a company of volunteers in Galena, and was drilling it for service. A few days afterwards he went with this company to Springfield, the capital of Illinois, and tendered his services to Governor Yates. The governor was quite willing to avail himself of the services of an educated officer like Grant, and desired that he should aid in organizing the troops volunteering in that state. Grant felt that he could be of more service to his country in the field, and that his duty required that he should go to the front and face the threatening danger. At the earnest request, however, of Governor Yates, who assured him that he should soon have a commission, he rendered valuable service in the organization and equipment of troops.

While awaiting the expected commission, he found leisure to go to Cincinnati, hoping that he might be offered a place on the staff of Major General McClellan, then in command of Ohio troops.* He twice called at the headquarters of McClellan, whom he had known in the army, but did not see that officer. It is hardly probable that Grant would have asked for such an appointment, even had he seen McClellan, for it was not in his nature to solicit office or promotion; and during his whole career not one of his promotions was sought by himself, or obtained through the influence of others by his desire. Nor did he even suggest the idea to any one that he desired an appointment on McClellan's

* General Badeau's Military History of U. S. Grant.

staff. Had it been offered to him he would have accepted it with alacrity, for he was ready to serve his country in any capacity, and had no undue opinion of his own abilities. It is fortunate for the country that McClellan did not offer him a staff appointment, for he would then have been in a subordinate position, where his characteristics and ability as an officer could not have been displayed; and had he remained in that position he would have suffered from the mistakes and policy of that general, and circumstances would thus have changed his whole military career.

Grant was probably disappointed, though he never expressed any such feeling; but his disappointment was the country's greatest gain. Returning to Springfield, he was very soon commissioned as colonel of the Twenty-first Regiment of Illinois volunteers, and with that regiment, early in June, he marched to Northern Missouri, and joined the forces of General Pope, who was engaged in putting down the guerrilla bands that infested that portion of the state. Ordered successively to different positions in this part of the country, he was faithfully discharging the arduous and not very agreeable duties of this kind of a campaign, when he was informed by the newspapers that he had been appointed a brigadier general. He received this appointment at the suggestion of Hon. E. B. Washburne, member of Congress from the Galena district; and it was all the more honorable to both parties, inasmuch as Mr. Washburne was but very slightly acquainted with Grant, and had nominated him, not from personal friendship, but because of the solid qualities which he was known to possess, his military education, and his good record in the old army. But neither Mr. Washburne, nor any one else at that time, knew the real ability of the man, or imagined the military genius which the opportunities of the war would reveal. He was commissioned on the 7th of August, to date from May 17, 1861, about the time he was appointed colonel by Governor Yates.

On the 1st of September Grant was assigned, by Major General Fremont, commanding the Western Department, to the command of the South-eastern District of Missouri, which included the southern part of Illinois and the western part of Kentucky and Tennessee, as far as the Union forces should advance. The governor of Kentucky, whose sympathy was more with the rebels than with the government, was endeavoring to have Kentucky maintain a neutral position in the contest; and all the rebels of that state, and not a few of those who claimed to be Union men, took the same ground. They sought to keep the national forces from their soil equally with the rebel forces—a measure which would have redounded entirely to the advantage of the rebels, who were collecting large forces in Tennessee, and were openly aided by their sympathizers in Kentucky. The real Union sentiment of that state was thus almost wholly repressed, and the state would have been soon controlled by the secessionists, who committed the grossest outrages upon Union men, and were preparing, under the guise of neutrality, to join the rebels.

The government did not recognize this neutrality, but claimed the right to move its troops to any part of the soil of the United States. General Grant was the first to exercise this right, and he exercised it promptly, knowing that it was *war*, and no game of politics, in which the country was engaged. He established his headquarters at Cairo, at the mouth of the Ohio, on the 4th of September, and at once set himself at work not only to strengthen that important point, but to secure the safety of his district, and commence operations against the enemy. On the day of his arrival at Cairo, the rebels were the first to violate the assumed neutrality of Kentucky by occupying Columbus, a strong position on the Mississippi. Grant saw the danger of this movement, and determined to check any further advance by at once entering Kentucky with the Union forces. He prepared to take possession of Paducah, at the confluence of the Tennessee River and the Ohio. Having notified General Fremont of his intention, and receiving no objection from that officer, he started for Paducah on the night of the 5th. He also notified the governor of Kentucky, and was rebuked by Fremont for holding any communication with state authorities, except through his superior officer. But Grant made no complaint of this, or any other disapproval of his course; for though he felt fully justified by his own calm judgment, he was a thorough soldier, and was always subordinate. He occupied Paducah, and secured it against a rebel force which was approaching, and against the treachery of malignant rebel residents. By the real Union men his movement was hailed with joy; and notwithstanding the complaints of those who loudly asserted the neutrality of Kentucky, that state was, by that prompt movement, secured to the Union cause. After the deed was done, Grant received permission from Fremont to attempt it "if he felt strong enough."

The seizure of Paducah first made Grant's name known to the country, though he did not receive the full credit to which he was entitled by his prompt action and the importance of the movement. The rebuke of his superior, on a matter of etiquette, served to derogate from his merit. This, however, had no effect upon Grant's zeal, and he continued to devote himself to the organization of his forces and the security of his district, with his usual quiet but untiring energy. He asked permission to attempt the capture of Columbus before it was made too strong by rebel fortifications; but no notice was taken of the request, and he was allowed to make no movement of importance.

In the early part of November, however, Fremont ordered Grant to make a demonstration towards Columbus, to prevent the rebels from sending reënforcements from that place to Price's army in South-western Missouri. This led to the battle of Belmont, Grant perceiving that an attack upon the rebels there would be the most effective way of preventing the rebel movements. His purpose was to destroy the rebel camp, disperse or capture their forces, and then retire before they could be reënforced from Columbus. He moved from Cairo the night of the 6th of November, with a little more than three thousand men, most of them new troops, and officered by men who had never seen an engagement. The troops were landed the next morning, about three miles from Belmont, which is opposite Columbus, on the Missouri shore. Marching towards that place, the enemy was encountered, and a heavy fight ensued, lasting four hours. Officers and men behaved nobly, and the rebels were driven step by step.

Grant, being the only officer who had seen service, found it necessary to direct even the details of movements, and was constantly in the skirmish line, encouraging his men by his presence, coolness, and bravery. His horse was shot under him, and he was constantly exposed to the enemy's fire. The rebels were driven to the bank of the river, and all their artillery and several hundred prisoners were captured.

Their success was too much for the Union troops. Officers and men joined at once in a general rejoicing, regardless of all discipline and the danger of rebel reënforcements from Columbus. But Grant was watchful, though almost powerless with his mob of an army; and perceiving that the enemy was sending more troops from Columbus, he ordered his staff to set fire to the rebel camp. Succeeding at last in securing some discipline, he ordered a return to the transports. But the defeated enemy had in the mean time been reënforced and re-formed, and they made an attempt to cut off the retreat. The undisciplined troops were somewhat disconcerted. A staff officer rode up to Grant, exclaiming, "We are surrounded!" "If that is so," coolly replied Grant, "we must cut our way out as we cut our way in." Riding to the front, he encouraged his men, saying, "We have whipped them once, boys, and we can do it again." The troops had already learned their commander's pluck, and making a vigorous attack they dispersed the rebel line.

With his inexperienced officers, Grant was obliged to attend to all the details of the retreat, and the collection of the wounded. The main body of the troops had reëmbarked on board the transports; and the reserves, which had been left to guard the boats, had also, through ignorance, embarked; but the general was still out attending to the execution of his orders, and awaiting the return of some of the detachments looking for the wounded. While thus engaged he found himself suddenly confronted by the rebels, who were still further reënforced, and not fifty yards distant. Fortunately he was not recognized as an officer; and after closely observing the position of affairs, he rode slowly away, finding it necessary to leave the parties which were still looking for the wounded. As he approached the river, he put spurs to his horse, and galloped hard to the bank, down which the animal slid on his haunches. The bullets were whistling about him, and the rebels were rapidly extending their line. The troops were all aboard, except the parties above named, and the boats were just leaving the landing when Grant thus appeared. A plank was put out from the last boat, and Grant rode aboard under a heavy, but happily an ineffectual, fire from the enemy. It appeared afterwards that the enemy had seen Grant, and that Polk, the rebel general, had called upon some of his troops to try their aim on him, though not knowing that he was an officer.

Grant had accomplished his purpose, though, owing to the want of discipline in his troops, not so quickly and effectually as he had desired. The enemy were well beaten at first; and again when, with more troops, he undertook to intercept the Union forces on their return to the boats, they were dispersed. When, with further reënforcements under Polk himself, they attacked the transports, the heavy fire of shell and grape from the gunboats yet again routed them with severe loss. With three thousand troops Grant had encountered about seven thousand rebels, and inflicted on them a loss one half greater than his own, besides the destruction of their camp and the capture of guns. Besides this he accomplished the principal object of the movement, which was to prevent Polk from sending reënforcements to Price.

But, as in the seizure of Paducah, Grant did not receive the credit which he deserved for this movement. Inexperienced soldiers, and correspondents of newspapers who did not know the object of the movement, were deceived by the sudden retreat and return of the troops to Cairo. Their representations, and perhaps those of an officer whose conceit and insubordination were afterwards the cause of trouble, led the country to believe that it was a failure. So far as the first victory was not so complete as it might have been, it was due to the wild exultation of the brave but undisciplined soldiers, and the stump speeches of their equally inexperienced officers. But the success was substantial; and Grant, with characteristic generosity, overlooked the faults of inexperience, and did not seek to excuse himself, or correct wrong impressions, by attributing even a partial failure to his subordinates. When asked why he did not report the colonels who had proved so inefficient in maintaining discipline, he replied, "These officers had never been under fire before; they did not know how serious an affair it was; they have had a lesson which they will not forget. I will answer for it, they will never make the same mistake again. I can see that they are of the right stuff, and it is better that I should suffer than the country should lose the services of such officers." This generous spirit towards subordinates and associates he has manifested through his whole career.

Immediately after the battle of Belmont, Major General Halleck superseded General Fremont in command of the Western Department. Grant was continued in command of his district, but for two months he was allowed to make no movement against the enemy. In the mean time the rebels occupied a strong line, extending from Columbus to Bowling Green, in Kentucky. Both these places, especially the former, were strongly fortified; and midway in the line, where the Tennessee and Cumberland Rivers are separated but ten or twelve miles, they had forts commanding these rivers. Thus all advance towards the rebel states by railroad or water was obstructed. In January, in obedience to instructions from Halleck, Grant sent two columns into Western Kentucky to prevent reënforcements being sent from Columbus to Buckner at Bowling Green. There was no engagement, but the object of the movement was accomplished, for the rebels did not send reënforcements to Buckner; and General Thomas defeated the enemy at Mill Spring, east of Bowling Green. The expedition led to the more important movements which first made General Grant famous in the war.

General C. F. Smith, an able officer, who commanded one of the columns sent into Western Kentucky, reported to Grant that the capture of Fort Henry, on the Tennessee, was feasible; and the latter went to St. Louis to propose to Halleck a movement against that post, and to obtain the latter's permission to undertake it. General Halleck, in a manner which he more than once afterwards assumed towards Grant, so sharply and hastily disapproved it, that the subject was at once dropped. Halleck appears at this time, and until after he was appointed general-in-chief, to have entertained a poor opinion of Grant's abilities, though he afterwards came to recognize them. But the advantage of capturing Fort Henry, opening the Tennessee to the rear of the rebel positions, though not apparent to McClellan and Halleck, was so impressed upon Grant's mind, that about the end of January he again applied to Halleck for permission to make the advance. Commodore Foote, commanding the naval force at Cairo, also wrote to Halleck recommending such a movement. The desired permission was obtained, and on the 2d of February Grant left Cairo with seventeen thousand men on transports, accompanied by seven gunboats under Commodore Foote. Making a reconnoissance himself on board one of the gunboats, so as to draw the fire of the rebel guns and ascertain their range, Grant landed his advance forces just out of range. This force, under McClernand, was to move out to the rear of the fort to intercept retreat and cut off reënforcements, while the gunboats undertook to reduce the fort on the river front. All Grant's forces were not up, but it was deemed important that there should be no delay, and he instructed McClernand that success might depend on the celerity of his movements. The troops moved from the river on the morning of February 6, and the gunboats at the same time moved up to attack the fort. Commodore Foote was not prepared for so speedy success as his heavy guns achieved; for after a fire of an hour and a half, all the rebel guns were silenced. The fort was surrendered while the troops were moving through the overflowed and almost impassable country to the position indicated. When they arrived at the rebel outworks in the rear, the enemy had already retreated towards Fort Donelson, on the Cumberland, and only a few men were captured in the fort. Pursuit failed to overtake them; but the most important success of opening the Tennessee was accomplished, and the gunboats went up the river, greatly to the terror of the rebel inhabitants of the interior of Tennessee.

But Grant, having taken the field, did not intend to content himself with the success so speedily achieved by the gunboats. He telegraphed to General Halleck, "Fort Henry is ours. . . . I shall take and destroy Fort Donelson on the 8th, and return to Fort Henry." Nothing had been said before about a movement against Fort Donelson; and it is not unlikely that such a proposition might have prevented the attack on Fort Henry, or delayed it till the Union forces were still stronger, and the rebels were also reënforced. Halleck, however, did not object, and Grant forthwith made his preparations to bring up additional forces, and to lay his plans for a joint land and naval attack. Prompt in his decision, he was also prompt and vigorous in his movements.

The rapid rise of the waters of the Tennessee, and the absence of the gunboats up that river, delayed operations for some days; but Grant in the mean time exerted himself to bring up reënforcements, and to mature his preparations. General Halleck seconded his efforts, though he gave no advice or encouragement for an advance. It was Grant's own plan in its conception and in its details. Before all the reënforcements which were ordered to his support had arrived, he determined to move, believing that it was important to act promptly. He therefore urged Flag Officer Foote to hasten his preparations, and offered such aid as was in his power, in order to get some gunboats up the Cumberland, to attack Fort Donelson on the river side. "Start as soon as you like," he wrote; "I will be ready to coöperate at any moment." Such was his promptness at all times. Other movements were never obliged to wait for him to be ready.

The gunboats at last being prepared, on the 11th of February Grant's forces moved from Fort Henry without tents or baggage, and with no supplies except ammunition and the rations contained in the soldiers' haversacks. The march was accomplished without obstruction, and the Union troops were in front of the rebel fort before night. On the 12th and 13th they were gradually advanced till the fort was well invested. No attack was made, owing to the non-arrival of the gunboats and reënforcements on the Cumberland, but there was constant skirmishing, and one or two heavy engagements by reconnoitring parties, while the artillery also commenced operations, and there were all the indications of a general battle. The weather grew intensely cold, snow fell, and the soldiers suffered much. They could build no fires in consequence of the nearness of the rebel pickets, with whom their was a sharp skirmish during the night. Though Grant felt keenly for the sufferings of his men, he knew that success depended upon his persistency, and that he could rely on the endurance of his troops. He must therefore hold on, in spite of the elements and the rebel strength, till the gunboats and reënforcements arrived, when he was confident of success. Before daylight on the 14th the boats arrived, and the reënforcements were put in position as soon as the condition of the country would permit.

An attack was made by the gunboats, and if it had been attended with even partial success, Grant was to have assaulted on the land side. But the boats were disabled, and suffered considerable loss in men, Flag Officer Foote himself being wounded. This was a serious disappointment to Grant, who had hoped to take the fort without a protracted siege. He was determined to take it, however, either by siege or assault, and never doubted the successful issue. In a conference with Foote, the latter stated that he could not renew the attack until he had been to Cairo to repair his gunboats, and urged Grant to remain quiet until he could return. Whether the latter, with his large reënforcements, would have been content to have taken this course, is uncertain; but the rebels themselves were not disposed to wait till they were more completely invested, and they accordingly massed their forces and made a heavy attack on Grant's right. Notwithstanding their long exposure and suffering from the severe storm of snow and sleet, the Union troops fought bravely. But the rebels had massed a superior force against the right, and they drove it back till checked by reënforcements. Even the latter were gradually pressed back, and the rebels seemed to have secured a dearly-bought success, though they were not able to break through the Union lines, as they desired.

Grant was returning from a conference with the disabled commodore when he was first informed of this desperate attack by the enemy, and its partial success. Ordering General Smith, who commanded the left, to hold himself in readiness, he hurried to the scene of conflict, and quickly ascertained the real condition of affairs. The stubborn bravery of his troops encouraged him, and he saw that the enemy had not accomplished their purpose, although they had pressed back his lines. From all the representations of his officers, he at once judged that the rebels had made a desperate assault for the purpose of cutting their way out and escaping. He caused some prisoners to be brought up for examination. They had on their knapsacks, and their haversacks were well filled.

"How many days' rations have you in your haversack?" inquired the general of one of the prisoners.

"Six," replied the prisoner.

"When were they served out?"

"Yesterday."

"Were all the troops served with the same rations?"

"They were."

The prisoners were removed, and further inquiry among his own officers satisfied Grant that the last statement was correct.

"Gentlemen," said he to the higher officers about him, "troops do not have six days' rations served out to them in a fort if they mean to stay there. These rebels mean to cut their way out, and that is what they have been trying to do, but didn't quite succeed." Then adding, with his characteristic determination, "Whichever party first attacks now will whip; and the rebels will have to be quick if they beat me," he put spurs to his horse and hurried to the left of his line.

The troops on his right had suffered severely, and were a little demoralized; but he knew their bravery and endurance, and that they would recover their spirit and be ready to endure still more if they were assured of victory. As he rode rapidly along, he gave hasty but cheering words of encouragement to them, which had the desired effect. His plans were quickly formed. He sent orders to Smith to make a vigorous assault, and directed McClernand and Wallace, on the right, to renew the battle as soon as Smith commenced his attack. At the same time he sent to Commodore Foote, requesting him to make a demonstration with such gunboats as were in condition to do so. In his note to Foote he wrote, "A terrible conflict ensued in my absence, which has demoralized a part of my command, and I think the enemy is much more so. If the gunboats do not appear, it will reassure the enemy, and still further demoralize our troops. I must order a charge to save appearances."

This was characteristic of Grant. He did not withdraw from the enemy's front at a critical moment because he had suffered a partial reverse, but he encouraged his own men by promptly assuming the offensive, and disheartened the enemy when exhausted by their desperate efforts. At Donelson, as on other fields where he acted with the same persistency and promptness, his tactics were successful. General Smith, who was a thorough soldier and a brave and skilful officer, made a brilliant assault; and after hard fighting his troops made their way through abatis and over rifle-pits inside the rebel intrenchments. At the same time the troops of McClernand and Wallace, encouraged by the words and confidence of Grant, renewed the battle and regained the ground they had lost earlier in the day. Night, however, came too soon for the entire success of the Union army. A half hour more of daylight and the fort would have been carried by storm. But without the cost of another assault the victory was won.

While the troops slept on the frozen ground which they had so bravely gained, the demoralized and beaten rebels were dreading a renewal of the battle, and their highest officers were preparing to desert the men who had fought under them. Floyd and Pillow, traitors to their cause and their comrades, as well as to their country, fled with as many troops as they could crowd into two steamers; and Buckner, the third in rank, was left to perform the disagreeable duty of surrendering. Buckner sent a messenger to General Grant, proposing an armistice and the appointment of commissioners to settle terms of capitulation. Grant's reply was prompt and decisive: "*No terms except unconditional and immediate surrender can be accepted. I propose to move immediately upon your works.*"

Buckner styled the terms "ungenerous and unchivalrous," but he was compelled to accept them. Grant, however, though never exhibiting a weak generosity towards the enemy, was never wanting in proper magnanimity. He rode to the headquarters of Buckner, who was a cadet with him at West Point, and allowed honorable terms to the prisoners, as Buckner himself voluntarily declared to his own soldiers. But in doing this he yielded no results of his brilliant victory. A most important rebel position was taken, with more guns than Grant had in his own forces, and fifteen thousand prisoners; while twenty-five hundred of the enemy were killed and wounded, and the three or four thousand fugitives who went with Floyd were completely demoralized.

The country needed such a victory to dispel the clouds of anxiety, and doubt, and impatience, which hung over the military horizon; and the army needed it to inspire hope and enthusiasm, which were well nigh extinguished by long delays and petty defeats. In itself, and in its important results, it had a glorious effect, and General Grant now first became known to the whole country, and received its gratitude. His prompt reply to Buckner gave to his initials the popular name of UNCONDITIONAL SURRENDER GRANT; and through his whole career he has maintained his title to that name, always exacting unconditional surrender from the enemies of his country.

## CHAPTER IV.

Appointed Major General of Volunteers. — Halleck's Notions. — General Smith. — Enemies and Unbelievers. — Misrepresentations unnoticed. — Misconception of Grant's Abilities. — Grant's Strategy. — "Up, Guards, and at them!" — Appreciative Friends. — Mr. Stanton and General Sherman. — Grant and Sherman contrasted. — Undeserved Censure by Halleck. — Grant's noble Reply. — His Conduct justified. — Up the Tennessee. — Pittsburg Landing. — Battle of Shiloh. — His Energy on the Field. — The Day saved by his obstinate Resistance. — Stragglers' Stories. — Grant's Ideas of Retreat. — He didn't intend to be beaten. — He assumes the Offensive. — Promptness and Energy. — His Orders given personally. — The Battle renewed. — Leads the Charge of Ohio Troops. — Victory. — Jealousy and Ignorance seek to deprive him of the Honors. — Halleck restive. — He takes Command. — Over-Caution. — Grant's Position. — His Sense of Wrong. — Grant and Sherman. — A Friendship fortunate for the Country. — Halleck called to Washington, and Grant resumes Command. — Defensive Operations. — "Honor to whom Honor is due."

IN recognition of his victory Grant was at once nominated by the President as a Major General of volunteers, and the nomination was promptly confirmed by the Senate, February 19, 1862. General Halleck, commanding the Western Department, and thus Grant's superior officer, appears to have ignored Grant, and in his letters and despatches speaks of "our" movements and "our" victory, without a word for him to whom belonged the honor of the victory. Halleck also recommended that Smith should be appointed a Major General, and said that to him belonged the credit of the victory; but he made no mention of Grant, who had not yet been promoted. Yet Halleck had nothing to do with the operations against Fort Donelson, except to send forward reënforcements. Grant was the projector of the movement as well as the commanding officer; and all the operations and attacks, including the assault by Smith's division, were ordered by him. Smith did not claim the honor, but declared that he only obeyed orders; and he was subsequently recommended by Grant, who was always generous to his subordinates, for promotion for his services. Smith was Grant's senior in years and in the service. He was commandant at West Point when Grant was a cadet, and the latter felt some delicacy in assuming command over his old instructor. But the veteran soldier was trained to subordination, and he soon put at rest all Grant's doubts, and carried out his orders with the greatest vigor and alacrity.

Grant appears to have had at that time, as at all times during the war and since, secret enemies, who depreciated his abilities and his achievements, and did not hesitate to circulate malignant calumnies concerning him. They were either jealous of his success, or were the enemies of the country, who did not wish to have the rebels conquered, and therefore hated an officer who was disposed to seek out the enemy and defeat him. These same enemies have followed him through all his career, no less since the war than during its continuance, only, as his reputation increased and he became firmly fixed in the affections of the people, their attacks have been more wary and insidious. Then there were others who detracted from his real merits because they did not understand the man or his purposes, and were governed by the misrepresentations of his enemies.

To correct misrepresentations, or counteract the machinations of enemies, Grant never made any effort. Obedient to orders, faithful to his duties, aiming always to serve his country in any capacity, never jealous of his fellow-officers, and never insubordinate, he neither found time nor showed any desire to set himself right before the government or the country, except by his deeds. He did not, like some generals, take pains to keep his "communications with the press" open. He did not divulge his plans to newspaper correspondents, nor boast of what he was going to do or what he had done. He did not encourage toadyism, nor listen to flatterers. He was reserved, and kept his own counsels as far as possible. He was therefore only known by what he accomplished; and because his plans were not known before, it was supposed that his successes were simply accidental, or due to his subordinates.

General Badeau, in his admirable "Military History" of General Grant, says, "It is impossible to understand the early history of the war, without taking it into account that neither the government nor its important commanders gave Grant credit for intellectual ability or military genius.

"His other qualities were also rated low. Because he was patient, some thought it impossible to provoke him; and because of his calmness, it was supposed he was stolid. In battle, or in campaigning, he did not seem to care or consider so much what the enemy was doing, as what he himself meant to do; and this trait, to enthusiastic and even brilliant soldiers, appeared inexplicable. A great commander, it was imagined, should be nervous, excitable, inspiring his men and captivating his officers; calling private soldiers by their names, making eloquent addresses in the field, and waving his drawn sword in battle. Great commanders had done all these things and won; and many men, who could do all these things, fancied themselves, therefore, great commanders. Others imagined wisdom to consist in science alone; they sought success in learned and elaborate plans, requiring months to develop, when the enemy was immediately before them; they manœuvred when it was time to fight; they intrenched when they should have attacked, and studied books when the field should have been their only problem.

"Grant was like none of these. If he possessed acquirements, he appeared unconscious of them; he made no allusions to the schools, and never hesitated to transgress their rules when the occasion seemed to him to demand it. So he neither won men's hearts by blandishments, nor affected their imaginations by brilliancy of behavior; nor did he seem profound to those who are impressed only by a display of learning."

But by his career, when uncontrolled by his superiors, he proved to these sceptics that he possessed both intellectual ability and military genius, and upset their preconceived notions of a great commander.

Grant did not have a very exalted opinion of "strategy" in the common acceptation of the word, though he was in fact a successful strategist and a master of grand tactics.

"I don't believe in strategy in the popular understanding of the term," he once said to one of his officers. "I use it to get up just as close to the enemy as is practicable with as little loss as possible."

"And what then?" asked the officer.

"Then? 'Up, guards, and at 'em!'" replied Grant, with more than his usual animation. And that was a fair general statement of his style of campaign.

Among those who early appreciated, if they did not do full justice to Grant's capacity, was Hon. Edwin M. Stanton, secretary of war, who thoroughly believed in Grant's "strategy" of seeking out the enemy and striking him. In a public announcement of the victory at Fort Donelson, he said that "the true organization of victory and military combination to end this war was declared by General Grant's message to General Buckner: '*I propose to move immediately on your works.*'" Possibly the implied rebuke to certain other commanders, contained in this, served to add to the prejudice of some against Grant. Mr. Stanton, however, never saw reason to change his estimate of Grant, and gave him the heartiest support through the war, till out of their official relations arose a cordial friendship.

General Sherman was another who was not slow to appreciate Grant's merits. He was in command at Cairo when the battle of Fort Donelson occurred, and labored with great zeal to send forward troops and supplies. He warmly congratulated Grant on his victory and his deserved promotion. To this Grant replied in a manner which shows his modesty, his generosity, and his patriotism: "I feel under many obligations to you for the kind terms of your letter, and hope that, should an opportunity occur, you will earn for yourself that promotion which you are kind enough to say belongs to me. I care nothing for promotion so long as our arms are successful, and no political appointments are made." The last words refer to the appointment of high officers from civil life, for political considerations alone, and not for military capacity, an instance of which Grant had already experienced. The friendship, which commenced with this correspondence, between these two distinguished officers is well known to the country. It has been of the most cordial character, free from all jealousy on the part of each, generous, self-sacrificing, and altogether worthy of these two greatest commanders of the war.

The two men possess the most opposite qualities in many respects, Sherman being nervous, impulsive, and excitable, while Grant is cool, firm, and imperturbable. Professor Mahan, a tutor at West Point while both were there, compares Grant to a powerful low-pressure engine, which condenses its own steam and consumes its own smoke, and which pushes steadily forward and drives all obstacles before it; and likens Sherman to a high-pressure engine, which lets off both steam and smoke with a puff and a cloud, and dashes at its work with resistless vigor.

After the victory at Fort Donelson, General Halleck, who, if he did not entertain a positive dislike for Grant, was not disposed to give him the credit he deserved, and was inclined to find fault with him, censured him for going to Nashville, — which Grant did for the sake of better understanding the position of affairs, — and complained that he did not make reports. This censure and complaint were utterly undeserved. But though Grant was thereby placed under a cloud for a time, and seemed likely to be superseded in his command of active operations, he made no complaint, but showed that subordination which he knew was essential to the service, and manifested his readiness to do all in his power for the good of the cause, and to carry out the orders of his superior. "I have done my very best to obey orders," he wrote, "and to carry out the interests of the service. If my course is not satisfactory, remove me at once. *I do not wish in any way to impede the success of our arms.*" Unselfish and patriotic, he had no thought for himself, but only for the cause. Finding that he was misrepresented by secret enemies, and still censured, he repeatedly asked to be relieved from duty until he could be placed right in the estimation of those higher in authority. But Halleck at last perceived that the country could not spare so true and subordinate an officer, and wrote to him, "Instead of relieving you, I wish you, as soon as your new army is in the field, to assume the immediate command, and lead it on to new victories." This was enough, and Grant at once showed his readiness, in spite of all calumnies, to "give every effort to the success of the cause." Halleck also made explanations to the War Department, which relieved Grant from the censure to which his (Halleck's) previous despatches had given rise.

Grant was thus justified by his own acts, as well as by the judgment of all true soldiers, on the only occasion when his conduct was called in question at Washington; though his unselfish patriotism was subjected to yet further trials by his immediate superior. He had already been appointed to the command of the District of West Tennessee, and when relieved from his unmerited disgrace, assumed command of the forces which were moving up the Tennessee, and the advance of which was encamped at Pittsburg Landing, awaiting reënforcements. The rebels, alarmed at the movements in Tennessee, were concentrating large forces at Corinth, Miss., and Buell was ordered to march from Nashville with forty thousand men to support Grant. The latter intended, as soon as these troops arrived, to advance on Corinth. But Buell's movements were slow, and the rebels determined to attack Grant's army before it was reënforced; and accordingly they advanced from Corinth, sixty thousand strong.

The position of the Union army at Pittsburg Landing was not selected by Grant, but by Smith before the former resumed command. It was naturally a good one, and it only required intrenchments to make it entirely safe till the time for an advance; but the western armies had not then learned the use of the pick and shovel. Grant made every effort to hurry forward the troops coming up from Cairo, and urged Buell to hasten on also. But the enemy, after various threatening movements, made their attack when the latter was a day's march away, and seemed in no great haste to reach the Tennessee, where he would be a subordinate.

The limits of this work will not allow the giving of the details of the battle of Shiloh, or of any of Grant's campaigns, but simply the narration of some of the leading events which show the ability and character of the general himself. Grant's headquarters were at Savannah, and he was preparing to go in search of Buell; but as soon as the attack was made, on the morning of April 6th, he hastened to the field, despatching an urgent message to Buell, and promptly making all the provision possible for the support of the troops already engaged. He anticipated the call for ammunition, and when cartridges were wanted they were already at hand, and a constant supply maintained. He was in all parts of the field, advising and commending his subordinates, constantly under fire, cool, energetic, and making unwearied exertions to maintain his position. At times he was vigorously engaged in sending deserters back to their regiments, and in organizing temporarily the numerous fugitives who crowded to the river with exaggerated stories of disaster. He sent again and again for Buell's advance to hurry forward, and for Lewis Wallace to hasten from Crump's Landing. But Buell's advance, slow to move, was yet a long way off, and Wallace strangely mistook the road, and did not arrive. Confident that with these reënforcements he could defeat the enemy, Grant held on with a tenacity which alone saved the day. The Union line was forced back more than a mile, but it was nowhere pierced. The enemy made desperate attacks; but the Union troops, encouraged by such officers as Grant and Sherman, fought like veterans, although many were new levies, and showed the dogged obstinacy which their commander seemed to inspire. The last desperate attacks upon the left of the Union line were met with such firmness, that the rebels were repeatedly thrown back until exhausted. At this time Buell's advance, under General Nelson, arrived, and some of his regiments were placed in position; but the enemy made only a feeble renewal of their efforts. *The day had been saved by Grant's obstinate resistance, and not by the arrival of Buell's troops.*

But all day, while the battle raged, the banks of the river had been crowded with stragglers from the front, some slightly wounded, some never in the battle, but all full of stories of surprise, overwhelming forces, terrible disasters, horrible slaughter, and all the exaggerations of men unused to battle, and of cowards who deserted their posts. Seen from the rear, it looked as if the contest was resulting in utter and irreparable defeat; and colored by these unworthy and untrue reports, the country was made to see the first day's battle at Shiloh as a disaster, which was only saved from utter completeness by Buell's arrival. Buell himself, who arrived in advance of his troops, apparently took a similar view, and as soon as he met Grant inquired, "What preparations have you made for retreating, general?" But he was quickly interrupted by Grant, who exclaimed, with firmness, "*I haven't despaired of whipping them yet!*" He knew how the brave men at the front were resisting the enemy, and he knew that if he held out through that day, the victory could be won the next, and so he never thought of retreat. Such was his determined spirit in all his campaigns, and in all his battles.

After the battle, it is said—though the anecdote is not so authentic as the above statement—that Buell, in criticising the position of Grant's army, with the Tennessee in their rear, again recurred to the question of retreat, and asked, "Where would you have retreated, general, if beaten?"

"I didn't intend to be beaten," was Grant's reply.

"But suppose, in spite of all your efforts, you had been defeated?"

"Well, there were the transports."

"But all your transports would not carry more than ten thousand men, and you had forty thousand."

"Well," replied Grant, "*they would have been sufficient for all that would have been left of us.*"

As soon as the rebels showed signs of exhaustion in their last efforts against his left, Grant was giving orders to assume the offensive on the morrow. He believed that, as at Fort Donelson, the condition of either side was such that the party first attacking would be successful. He would then have at least one division of Buell's army, and Wallace's division, to strengthen him, and he was confident of success. His preparations were made promptly and decisively. His shattered brigades were reorganized, stragglers were returned to their places, and ample supplies brought up. Buell's army, as it arrived, was placed in position on the left, and Wallace's division on the right, and by early morning the new line was formed. Grant gave his orders personally to each division commander, and after completing his plans, he lay down on the ground, with the stump of a tree for a pillow, and slept soundly in spite of the raging storm. The attack was made this time by the Union troops, and the rebels were beaten back. The battle was severe, though not so fierce as on the previous day. The rebels retired slowly, but were at last driven from the field, and retreated rapidly towards Corinth. Grant's plans were carried out, and he was ever active on the field in directing new movements. Seeing a portion of his line, in front of an important position, struggling unsuccessfully and about to give way, he ordered up an Ohio regiment, which was passing not far distant, and himself led them to support the wavering troops. Recognizing their general, these men charged with great enthusiasm, while he shared their exposure, and encouraged them with his presence. The wavering troops also recognized him, and closing up their ranks, they joined, with loud cheers, in the charge, which drove the enemy from their position, and achieved the final success of the contest.

Jealousy and ignorance would again have deprived Grant of the honor of victory. He was supposed to have been hopelessly defeated the first day, and the success of the second day was supposed to be due to Buell and his army. But neither was true, as all official records, of both the Union and rebel forces, and the testimony of unprejudiced soldiers, show. Moreover, had the army of General Buell been as ready to endure and persist as were General Grant's own troops, the victory would have been more complete. But Buell's officers considered their men too much exhausted to pursue the routed foe; and the real victory, which Grant desired to achieve, was thus lost. But what was accomplished is due to the ability and persistency of Grant.

General Halleck, seeing his subordinates winning the laurels of the war, grew somewhat restive; and having formed a grand strategical plan of the campaign, desired naturally to assume command of his forces in the field. He did so, and superseded Grant, who, though nominally second in command, was practically ignored, and placed in a very awkward and unpleasant position. The misrepresentations of jealousy and ignorance had their effect upon Halleck, and he seemed to believe that Grant had hopelessly failed at Shiloh.* The latter was not consulted, and orders were issued by Halleck direct to the corps commanders, instead of being sent through Grant. The spade and pick were now brought into requisition, as if in contrast to the only omission of Grant in taking position at Pittsburg Landing. For weeks the grand army under Halleck was throwing up breastworks, advancing a short distance and again throwing up breastworks, till it had dug its way almost into Corinth, advancing fifteen miles in six weeks. The rebels meanwhile were equally busy in erecting defences at Corinth.

To some able officers, and among them General Grant, it appeared that there was a surer and quicker way of carrying the rebel position, and defeating the rebel army before it escaped. But when Grant ventured to suggest it, Halleck scouted it in an insulting manner. Grant had hitherto borne his disagreeable position with patience and entire subordination, as became a good soldier and a patriotic, unselfish man, trusting that time would bring all things right. But this indignity was almost past bearing. He felt it keenly, and was much depressed; but he showed no insubordination, made no complaints, and sought no sympathy from his fellow-

* General Badeau's excellent work, "The Military History of Ulysses S. Grant," throws new light on this battle, and shows, by official documents and the testimony of General Sherman and others, that Grant not only did not fail, but that he was entitled to the highest honor for his ability and persistency.

officers, which might have affected the efficiency of the army. He simply remarked to his chief of staff that Halleck had deeply wronged him.

One day General Sherman bolted into Grant's tent, and found him suffering under his sense of wrong. He inquired the cause of this unusual manifestation of feeling. Grant then, for the first time, spoke at length of his position, and the indignities he had suffered, and concluded by saying, "The truth is, I am not wanted here. The country has no further use for me, and I am about to resign and go home."

"No, you are not!" replied Sherman, in his nervous and impatient manner; "you are going to do nothing of the sort. The country has further need of you, and you must stay here and do your duty, in spite of these petty insults."

Sherman's earnest manner, generous sympathy, and cheering words prevailed with Grant, and encouraged him to stay. Fortunate was it for the country, that at this critical moment of his career Grant had so appreciative, true, and outspoken a friend.

When Corinth was evacuated by the rebels, and entered by the Union troops after their six weeks of fruitless toil, it was apparent that Grant's plan would have secured the capture not only of Corinth, but the greater part of the rebel army. The inefficient pursuit which followed, under the direction of Buell, assumed the form of seventy thousand men acting on the defensive, against twenty thousand rebels retreating from them! This barren issue of the "siege of Corinth" served to distract attention from the alleged mistakes of Shiloh, and Grant was no longer subject to the calumnies which had been heaped upon his capacity as a general, and his habits as a man.

Halleck was soon after called to Washington as general-in-chief, and Grant resumed his former command; not, however, till Halleck had offered it to Colonel Robert Allen, a quartermaster, who had the good sense to decline it. Buell's army had already gone towards Chattanooga, and Grant's army was still further depleted by the departure of four divisions to reënforce the former. Grant was, therefore, compelled to act entirely on the defensive, an irksome duty for him; and his task was the difficult one of guarding several important points against an enemy who could readily concentrate at any one of them a force equal to his entire command. He strengthened the defences of Corinth, while he narrowly watched the threatening movements of the rebels, and proved himself active and prudent in a defensive campaign, though his genius was for offensive operations. He would have defeated the rebels at Iuka if his plans had been carried out; but Rosecrans, who commanded one of the columns moving against the enemy at that place, was slower than he promised to be, which caused a necessary detention of the other column, under Ord, and communication being difficult, the attacks were not well timed. The enemy effected his retreat by a road which Rosecrans was expressly ordered to hold, but which he failed to occupy.

Afterwards the rebels, combining their forces, attacked Corinth, to which place Grant had hurried Rosecrans, and made other provisions for its defence. With the aid of the strengthened fortifications Rosecrans made a gallant defence, and repulsed the enemy with heavy loss; but he failed to pursue the demoralized forces of the rebels until it was too late. Grant was somewhat chagrined at this, for his plans always contemplated the prompt following up of a success until its full benefits were reaped. The result, however, was advantageous to the Union cause, and Grant's district was relieved from apprehensions of a renewal of important movements on the part of the enemy. For the defence of Corinth Rosecrans received deserved commendation; but more was due to Grant than partial observers allowed. His were the plans by which success was achieved, and had they been carried out, would have resulted in a more complete victory.

## CHAPTER V.

Vicksburg. — General McClernand's Schemes. — Grant's Purposes. — The Lessons of a rebel Raid. — Grant and the Secession Women. — McClernand's Insubordination and Braggadocio. — The Difficulties of operating against Vicksburg. — Grant's Persistency and Resources. — The Canal, Lake Providence, and Yazoo Pass. — The Country impatient. — Plots to remove him. — President Lincoln's Reply. — The final and successful Plan. — Opposition. — Grant assumes the Responsibility. — Brilliant Operations. — Jackson, Champion Hill, and the Big Black. — The Assault on Vicksburg, and the Siege. — Strategy and Vigor. — Vicksburg reduced. — Grant's Interview with Pemberton. — "Unconditional Surrender" again. — Thirty thousand Prisoners, and one hundred and seventy-two Cannon. — The public Joy. — President Lincoln's Letter. — General Halleck's Acknowledgment. — Grant's modest Dignity, and the sullen Discourtesy of Rebels. — Grant's Confidence of Success. — His Persistency dashes the Hopes of a rebel Woman. — His unwearying Labors and Efforts. — Care for his Troops. — His well-earned Reputation.

VICKSBURG, which will be forever associated with the name of Grant, was the scene of achievements which confirmed him in the estimation of his countrymen, and established his reputation as a general above the reach of the detractions of jealousy and misrepresentation. While Grant was engaged in defending his district of West Tennessee from the threatened invasion of the superior forces of the enemy, McClernand, who had been his subordinate, and was one of the political appointments which he had deprecated, was in Washington, endeavoring to obtain an independent command. It was very desirable that the Mississippi River should be opened its entire length. The Union forces had opened it to Memphis and below, but at Vicksburg the rebels had strong fortifications, and entirely commanded the river between that place and Port Hudson, thus maintaining their communications between the west and the east, and drawing large supplies from Louisiana and Texas. McClernand proposed to open this part of the river, and persuaded President Lincoln to authorize him to organize a force of the new troops from the west for that purpose. He imagined himself fully equal to the undertaking, talked boastfully, claimed the expedition as his original conception, and desired the sole command, with the idea that he should have the sole honor of its success. General Halleck, however, and others, had no such exalted opinion of McClernand's abilities as an officer, and he was allowed to organize the expedition subject to General Grant's direction. Halleck seemed to have more faith in Grant than formerly, or at least placed him far above McClernand as a soldier. He atoned for his former injustice by allowing Grant great freedom of action, and heartily aiding him in all his plans.

But McClernand had no patent right to such a movement. It had formed a part of Halleck's grand plan of operations when he was commander of the Western Department; and Grant had long ago had his eye on Vicksburg as an objective, towards which he would have advanced had his forces been sufficient. Before McClernand got ready to take command of his expedition, Grant sent Sherman, with all the troops collected at Memphis, except a sufficient garrison, down the river to commence operations, and entered earnestly into the movement which was to be under his general direction.

As McClernand's new levies arrived, they were sent to the same destination. Grant at the same time penetrated Mississippi, with the view of coöperating in the rear of Vicksburg. But his forces, though he had accomplished much, were insufficient to hold his long line of railroad communication, and still make advances. The rebels were wary, and, avoiding battle, suddenly cut his communications, and destroyed a large quantity of supplies, and he was obliged to fall back; while Sherman made an unsuccessful attack on the rebel position on the Yazoo. But the cutting of his communications taught Grant to subsist his army on the enemy's country. The rebels were rejoicing over this disaster to the Union cause, which they exaggerated, and fancied that the national troops must either starve where they were, or retreat, demoralized and beaten, an easy prey for Forrest's active cavalry.

Some rebel women came one day to Grant's headquarters, smiling with exultation at the news they had heard. They thought to taunt him, "in a genteel way," with his loss, and, as they supposed, his hopeless condition.

"What will you do, general," asked one, "now that you have lost Holly Springs, and your soldiers will have nothing to eat?"

The general noticed, without appearing to, the glances exchanged by his visitors, and the taunting tone, which was but half concealed, and he quickly replied, —

"My soldiers will find plenty to eat in your barns and storehouses."

The exultant smiles of his visitors were quickly changed to looks of astonishment and alarm.

"You would not rob us! You would not take from non-combatants!" they cried.

"A commander's first duty is to provide for his troops," replied the general, blandly. "Your friends destroyed my supplies, and I must take others wherever they may be found."

Remonstrances could not prevail, nor indignant protests, nor harmless threats, nor angry tears. The troops must be fed, and the orders were given to seize all necessary supplies. Grant was now convinced, if he had not been at an earlier stage of the war, that the rebels, who wickedly began the rebellion, and prosecuted it with such obstinacy, hatred, and cruelty, should be made to feel the rigors of war, and that treacherous and malignant non-combatants — those innocents whose "sufferings" Franklin Pierce bewailed — should not be spared. So the country was stripped, and the army was fed. The rebels paid dearly for this raid on Grant's communications, not only there, but throughout the South wherever the Union armies marched, for the lesson which he then learned was afterwards thoroughly and justly practised.

When McClernand took command, he not only lacked the confidence of experienced soldiers, but he manifested insubordination, with overweening conceit criticised the orders of his superior, claimed the expedition as his own, and sought to establish his independence of Grant. His conduct was so offensive, and so endangered the success of the movement, that Grant was authorized to name another commander, or to assume the command himself. To avoid unpleasant results, which might have arisen from superseding McClernand by Sherman, to whom he wished to give the command, he assumed it himself, and retained McClernand in command of his own corps. But the latter, while not a very efficient officer, was still insubordinate and troublesome, boastful and obnoxious to his fellow-officers. Finally his spirit of braggadocio led him to exaggerate what he was doing during one of the fierce assaults in the rear of Vicksburg, to claim successes which he had not gained, and to ask for support which involved an unnecessary sacrifice of life. And to crown this, he published a bombastic address to his corps, in which he recounted all its gallant deeds to his own glory, and the disparagement of other corps and commanders. This unsoldierly conduct justly incensed other officers, and McClernand was at once relieved of his command, which he had obtained through political influence, and in the exercise of which the good of the country was made subordinate to his own glorification. But for Grant's patience and forbearance, he would have been sooner relieved for other reasons.

The movement against Vicksburg was one of the greatest importance. Its object was to open the Mississippi, in order not only to secure that majestic line of communication with the sea, and with the Union forces at its mouth, but to divide the rebel confederacy in twain, and to cut off the rebel armies in the east from one of their chief sources of supply. It was a movement full of difficulties, for it was a position of great natural strength, affording no vantage-ground for an attack, and it had been industriously fortified. The rebels knew its importance to them, and they spared no pains to make it secure. At the first indications of a movement against it, they extended and strengthened its defences, and concentrated their forces so as to be able to present, at any point of attack, numbers at least equal to the assailants.

General Grant believed from the first that the only way of capturing Vicksburg was by an attack in the rear, or a siege. Such had been his plans before the expedition down the river had been determined upon; and when his communications were cut, had he known what he then learned by experience, and what was then first tried by any considerable force, — that he could subsist an army on the enemy's country, — he would have moved promptly on Vicksburg. But the river expedition was now the favorite one with the government, and at this time, perhaps, the most advantageous one, and he bent all his energies to secure its success, aiming still to get to the rear of the rebel position. It was impossible to carry the enemy's works in front, or on their flank, an attack at the only practicable point, on the Yazoo, having already failed; and it was equally impossible to pass the rebel batteries on the river with a sufficient number of transports and gunboats in order to flank them on the south. The problem was, therefore, somewhat difficult in theory as well as in practice.

The year previous, a Union force, under the command of General Williams, had been sent up from New Orleans by General Butler, with a part of Admiral

Farragut's fleet, and being unable to pass Vicksburg, had commenced cutting a canal across the neck of land formed by the bend in the river opposite Vicksburg, with the view of turning the waters of the Mississippi, and securing a safe passage, while leaving Vicksburg some miles inland. Without being too confident of success, Grant ordered this work to be completed on a larger scale and in a more effective manner. He always felt that it was essential to keep his men actively employed; and even if this canal did not enable the fleet to pass down below Vicksburg, it occupied the attention and encouraged the hopes of the troops. The work was pushed forward with vigor; but it took months to bring it near completion, and then a rapid rise in the river broke through the embankment of the canal and overflowed the country, and the work did not answer its purpose.

But Grant had not been idly awaiting the result of this experiment. He was busy in seeking other practicable routes by which he could reach the position he desired. As soon as he took command, he gave orders for cutting a way from the Mississippi to Lake Providence on the west, from which it was hoped steamers might pass into the Tensas, and thence into the Red River, and a passage thus be opened for communication with Banks, who was to coöperate from New Orleans in the opening of the river. At about the same time he sent an expedition to explore on the eastern side of the Mississippi, and to open, if possible, a practicable passage through Yazoo Pass and Steele's Bayou. At one time the latter route promised to be practicable, and to enable Grant to flank the rebel works on the

Yazoo, and reach the high land in the rear of Vicksburg. But unexpected obstacles, natural and artificial, were encountered; and though the novel and remarkable movement was prosecuted with vigor, and caused serious loss and alarm to the rebels, it was found at last to be unavailing.

While Grant was making all these efforts to solve the problem before him, the country, ignorant of the difficulties and the measures taken to overcome them, became impatient. There was a clamor for his removal, prompted in part by jealousy, and in part by ignorance and impatience. This feeling at Washington, and at the North, suggested all sorts of rumors and misrepresentations about Grant, the condition of his troops, and everything which could affect his character as a general. Great efforts were consequently made to remove him; and among those who were using every exertion to accomplish this was General McClernand, who desired and expected to have the command himself. How much of the misrepresentation of Grant and his efforts is due to that scheming subordinate and his friends, may be imagined. He would probably have succeeded but for the good will and firmness of President Lincoln, who even then believed in Grant. To one of those who urged Grant's removal the President said, decidedly, "I rather like the man. I think we'll try him a little longer." Secretary Stanton, too, "rather liked the man," and he was not removed to give place to incompetency and bombast. Amid all this clamor and misrepresentation, Grant patiently and earnestly discharged his duties, seeking success against the enemy for the sake of the country, rather than wasting efforts for the sake of himself. So through his whole career, while there was an enemy of his country in his front, he did not turn back to fight his personal enemies in the rear. And never did he undertake to defend himself against the misrepresentations and plots of unscrupulous men, until in himself the safety and welfare of the country were assailed, and the fruits of all his victories were endangered.

But Grant's resources were not exhausted. He had yet another plan, to which, from the beginning, he had anticipated he might resort when the waters had sufficiently subsided. This was to move his army, which was now large and well organized, partly by water through the bayous on the west side of the river, and partly by a wagon road to New Carthage, and thence across the Mississippi below Warrenton, or to a point still farther down the river, and thence across to Grand Gulf. Admiral (then Commodore) Porter at the same time was to run by the rebel batteries with several of his gunboats, and some transports laden with supplies. These gunboats and transports, with such small steamers as could pass through the bayous, were to transport the troops across the river, and a movement was then to be made to the rear of Vicksburg. To this movement Grant's most trusted and able officers, such as Sherman and McPherson, were strongly opposed, as dangerous in the extreme. The army, they represented, would abandon its base of supplies, and would be entirely cut off from the North and all aid in case of any failure; and if not entirely successful, for which the chances were far from equal, the movement would be disastrous. But Grant had weighed the subject well, was confident of success, and quietly assuming the responsibility, without holding any council of war, adhered to his plan, and issued orders for its execution.

The movement was successfully made, and attended with the most brilliant results. The gunboats, and most of the transports, passed the batteries at night without serious damage; the troops moved promptly, under Grant's personal direction, and soon reached New Carthage. There, however, there was a delay on account of McClernand's inefficiency, and Commodore Porter was constrained to urge the immediate presence of Grant at the front. Further examination showing that it was advisable, in consequence of McClernand's delay, to cross the Mississippi at a point below Grand Gulf, which was strongly fortified, General Grant, upon assuming immediate command, moved down from New Carthage to a point opposite Bruinsburg. There the troops were transported across the river by the steamers and gunboats, and established themselves on the Mississippi side, and compelled the evacuation of Grand Gulf. Then Grant, sending his pithy despatch, "You may not hear from me again for several days," cut loose from his base, and commenced his brilliant campaign. With skilful movements, which deceived the enemy, he marched to Jackson, skirmished, fought battles, captured Jackson, the capital of Mississippi, and then rapidly marched back to the rear of Vicksburg, defeating the rebels at Champion Hill and the Big Black, and driving them at last within the defences of their stronghold. The rebel forces were driven in dismay from Jackson, and their supplies captured and destroyed; and as the army moved towards Vicksburg, the country was laid waste, and the railroad destroyed, so as to prevent or impede any rebel movement for the relief of Vicksburg.

It was one of the most successful and brilliant operations of modern warfare, and reflected the highest credit on Grant's military capacity. It was the conception of military genius, and was carried through by that confidence which is inspired by genius. Grant's army was now placed where he desired it—in front of the enemy, who was thus cut off from reënforcements and supplies. Another brilliant move and gallant contest, and communication was opened with the Mississippi above Vicksburg, and a base of supplies established. Grant was not disposed to commence the slow operations of a regular siege until he had attempted to carry the enemy's works by assault. He was especially induced to do this because of the danger of a movement upon his rear if he waited too long, believing the importance of Vicksburg to the rebels might lead them even to abandon other points, in order to concentrate a large army for its relief. But finding that the rebel works were too strong to be carried by assault, he commenced regular siege operations, guarding, by a strong force in his rear, against the advance of Johnston, who was collecting all the troops he could for the relief of the beleaguered city. The operations of this force in the rear, under the immediate command of Sherman, were brilliant and effectual. The country, for a great distance, was stripped of supplies, and every important point was guarded, so that Johnston was unable to make any successful movement. The siege operations, in the mean time, progressed with vigor. By the disposition of Grant's forces, and the activity of the gunboats on the river, Vicksburg was completely cut off from supplies and reënforcements. The Union army slowly but surely advanced, siege guns were mounted, and the rebel fortifications and the city were continually shelled. The approaches at last reached the enemy's lines; one or two important rebel works were mined, assaulted, and captured, and the rebels, reduced to quarter rations, harassed and worn out by fatigues, at last, in despair, were obliged to yield.

On the 3d of July, Pemberton, the rebel commander, proposed an armistice and the appointment of commissioners to arrange for capitulation, in order "to save the further effusion of blood." Grant declined to appoint commissioners, and informed Pemberton that he could stop the further effusion of blood "by an *unconditional surrender* of the city and garrison," and that he could offer no other terms. An interview subsequently took place between the two commanders in front of the lines.

When they met, Pemberton inquired, somewhat abruptly, what terms would be allowed him.

"The terms named in my letter of this morning," replied Grant.

"If that is all," declared Pemberton, haughtily, "then this conference may as well terminate, and hostilities be resumed at once."

"Very well," said Grant, quietly; and he turned away, knowing that the enemy would soon be at his mercy.

But Bowen, Pemberton's subordinate, proposed that

he and General Smith, who accompanied Grant, should confer together on terms, and report to their superiors. While those two officers conferred together, Grant and Pemberton paced to and fro, conversing. Pemberton, nervous and dispirited, though insolent in manner, plucked straws to gnash his teeth upon; while Grant, quiet, imperturbable, and firm, calmly smoked his cigar, and as calmly spoke, taking no notice of his opponent's ill temper.

The terms proposed by Bowen were so utterly inadmissible as to elicit a smile from Grant, who promptly rejected them, and promised to send his ultimatum in writing, and the conference ended. Grant summoned a council of war, the only one he ever called, and asked the opinions of his officers. Always self-reliant, and ready to assume his proper responsibility, he evidently did not believe that in war there was safety in a multitude of counsel. In this case none of the terms proposed by his subordinates met with his approbation; but without any discussion he immediately dictated his own terms, which were in the main simply such as had been arranged by a cartel between the national and rebel authorities. The rebels were compelled to accept them or fare worse; and that was the position in which Grant always aimed to place the enemy.

On the 4th of July, Vicksburg, with its hundred and seventy cannon, and its thirty thousand rebel troops,* was formally surrendered, and a portion of the victorious army entered the city. The Mississippi was opened, for Port Hudson was immediately surrendered,

* One hundred and seventy-two cannon and thirty-one thousand six hundred men.

as a consequence of the capture of Vicksburg, and the long-desired and important object of this campaign was attained: the Father of Waters rolled "unvexed to the sea." The joyful news was flashed by telegraph through the country, and, added to the victory at Gettysburg, made that birthday of the country triply glorious and happy for the loyal people. The popular gratitude to Grant was freely expressed, and he was now recognized, by people, government, and soldiers, as, beyond all question, an able general, who, by brilliant movements, as well as indomitable energy, had secured victory unsurpassed in magnitude and importance by any hitherto achieved. President Lincoln, who had watched the progress of the operations against Vicksburg with the deepest interest, in a letter characterized by the honest frankness which was one of his prominent traits, wrote to Grant, —

"MY DEAR GENERAL: I do not remember that you and I ever met personally. I write this now as a grateful acknowledgment for the almost inestimable service you have done the country. I wish to say one word further. When you first reached the vicinity of Vicksburg, I thought you should do what you finally did — march the troops across the neck, run the batteries with the transports, and thus go below; and I never had any faith, except a general hope that you knew better than I, that the Yazoo expedition, and the like, could succeed. When you got below, and took Port Gibson, Grand Gulf, and vicinity, I thought you should go down the river and join General Banks; and when you turned northward, east of the Big Black, I thought it was a mistake. I now wish to make the personal acknowledgment that you were right, and I was wrong."

Other men, soldiers and civilians, ignorant of the difficulties and obstacles to be encountered, had made plans for taking Vicksburg, but few were so frank as President Lincoln, who, from that hour, had the fullest confidence in Grant, and gave him his hearty support.

General Halleck, who had been so slow to acknowledge Grant's ability, but who was thoroughly competent to judge of the merits of a campaign accomplished, wrote, "Your narrative of the campaign, like the operations themselves, is brief, soldierly, and in every respect creditable and satisfactory. In boldness of plan, rapidity of execution, and brilliancy of routes, these operations will compare most favorably with those of Napoleon about Ulm."

When, on the 4th of July, Grant rode into the captured city, it was without any ostentatious parade, or any exhibition of triumph. The rebel soldiers stared at him curiously, as if they wondered how so unpretending a man could be a great general. Stopping at Pemberton's headquarters, he dismounted, and alone entered the porch of the house, neither guard nor officer receiving him. There sat Pemberton and his rebel officers, occupying all the seats; but, though they recognized him, not one of these polished scions of chivalry had the grace to offer him a chair, nor to give him a glass of cold water when he asked for it. It was, however, a sullen incivility and exhibition of bad temper, which had little effect on Grant. Though he wore no air of haughty triumph, he was conscious of his victory; but he could pardon something to chagrin and wounded vanity; and while the vanquished Pemberton and his fellows continued sitting, the victor stood, quietly and courteously talking, till his business with the rebel chief was finished.

Through all the long campaign against Vicksburg, Grant had felt sure of ultimate success. His greatest anxiety — which, even then, did not amount to a doubt — was when he was contending against unnumbered difficulties and obstacles in his efforts to reach the enemy, and the country was becoming impatient at the tedious delays. But when he found that his long-contemplated movement could be made, he was no longer anxious, except to get his troops forward. He never doubted the result; he was confident of victory. His confidence then, as in all his campaigns, amounted almost to fatalism; but it was a confidence born not of blind egotism, or a superstitious belief in inevitable destiny, but of indefatigable effort and unyielding tenacity of purpose. When Sherman and McPherson advised against the movement, he was too confident to listen to their fears. When McClernand's inefficiency gave the rebels time to baffle his first plans, his confidence was not abated; but changing the details, he was never doubtful of reaching the end he aimed at. An incident during the siege illustrates the same confidence, and reveals its character.

As he was one day riding around his lines, he stopped for water at a house in which, notwithstanding its exposure, a rebel woman continued to live. Like most of her class, she was a bitter hater of the Yankees, and a thorough believer in the chivalry. Learning who Grant was, she thought she would taunt him by asking, —

"Do you expect ever to get into Vicksburg, general?"

"Certainly," replied the general, quietly but decidedly.

"I wonder when!" said the dame, with an evident sneer.

"I cannot tell exactly *when* I shall take the town," said the general, with a little more decision than before; "*but I mean to stay here till I do, if it takes me thirty years.*"

The woman subsided. Such Yankee persistency and confidence dashed her spirits and her hopes. But she saw the general's promise kept without waiting thirty years.

While Grant was thus confident of the result from his tenacity of purpose, he labored indefatigably to secure it. Cautious, vigilant, active, his orders to his subordinates were promptly and explicitly given; and when fairly in the field, every considerable movement contributed to secure the object in view. The experience of the campaign developed his military genius, and proved him a great general in his ability to move and feed troops, as well as in the grand tactics of the field. His army was prompt and rapid in its movements, and always well supplied; and he attended so closely to the details of these matters, that, without the slightest effort or desire to make himself popular, he secured the attachment of his men. But he did not content himself with simply seeing that they were furnished with supplies; he looked well after the wounded and sick, and protected all against the extortions of sutlers and steamboat captains, and other classes of vampyres that followed the army. Plain, quiet, and unassuming, but self-reliant, brave, and cool in the midst of danger, he was just the man to inspire the confidence, if not the enthusiasm, of the army under his command. He had thus, at the close of this brilliant campaign, established with the government, in the army, and before the world, a reputation as a general more solid than that of any other officer in the country.

## CHAPTER VI.

Appointed Major General in the regular Army. — His military Genius developed by the War. — His comprehensive Ideas of the Rebellion. — A true Representation of the Policy of the Government. — A Believer in Emancipation. — An Opponent of Trade with the Rebels. — Speculators and illegal Traders at a Discount. — Recognized as a great Leader and "the Coming Man." — Grant's Plans after the Capture of Vicksburg. — The Necessity of postponing them. — Visits New Orleans. — Accident and Injury. — Critical Position of Rosecrans. — Grant called to Cairo. — Meets Secretary Stanton. — New and important Command. — Confidence of the Government. — Assumes Command. — Affairs at Chattanooga. — Grant's prompt and energetic Preparations. — Journey to Chattanooga. — Triumph of Will over physical Weakness and Difficulties. — Extent of his Command. — Energy and Administrative Ability. — Chattanooga relieved, and the Army encouraged. — Burnside. — Grant's Purpose to attack Bragg. — Impatient of Delays. — The Battle of Chattanooga. — Fought directly under Grant's Orders. — His Headquarters. — The Crisis and the Charge. — Grant's Confidence. — "They'll do it." — The Victory. — Grant at the Front. — His Watchfulness. — Complete Defeat of the Enemy. — Pursuit. — "One of the most remarkable Battles in History." — Recognition of Grant's Services. — Modesty of the great Republican Soldier.

SOON after the capture of Vicksburg, and in recognition of his distinguished services, Grant was appointed a Major General in the regular army, his commissions hitherto having been in the volunteers. With his characteristic generous regard for his subordinates, he recommended many of them for promotion; and Sherman and McPherson were, at his request, appointed brigadier generals in the regular army. All

Grant's promotions had been won by merit and eminent services. He had risen in rank without personal or political influence, and in spite of the opposition and prejudices of men whose opinions essentially controlled the government.

The war had gradually developed his military capacity, and he had grown in his abilities with each new difficulty and each new campaign. Already the most successful and the ablest general in the Union army, in the coming campaigns he was destined to surpass himself, and to secure still more the gratitude and admiration of his country and the respect of all the world.

General Grant had grown not only in military capacity, but he had grown more comprehensive in his ideas of the rebellion. In all the army the government had no better representative of its policy. For Grant had always shown the most exact subordination, and declared his purpose to be, to carry out in all cases the orders of his superiors. He had learned what the rebellion was, and he had learned that it was necessary to deal with it with the utmost rigor. Never having been an abolitionist, he yet had learned that slavery was the cause, the object, and the strength of the rebellion, and he not only felt no scruples in striking it down, but earnestly carried out the emancipation policy. He did not hesitate to avow, still more decidedly than by passive obedience to orders, his sentiments on this subject, and in a letter to some loyal men of Memphis, who tendered him a public reception in 1863, he wrote, "I thank you, too, in the name of the noble army which I have the honor to command. It is composed of men whose loyalty is proved by their deeds of heroism and their willing sacrifices of life and health. They will rejoice with me that the miserable adherents of the rebellion, whom their bayonets have driven from this fair land, *are being replaced by men who acknowledge human liberty as the only true foundation of human government*."

When the policy of enlisting negroes in the army was adopted by the government, he gave it his hearty support, and he was not slow to acknowledge the bravery and discipline of the colored troops, nor to secure to them the full rights of soldiers.

He gave his hearty concurrence and his ready obedience to all orders and every policy which was calculated to weaken or break down the rebellion. But to such orders as he believed would indirectly aid and strengthen the enemy, he frankly presented his objections; and thus he urged cogent reasons against the policy of opening trade with the rebels for the sake of cotton, though he declared, *what was always his rule of action*, "No theory of my own will ever stand in the way of executing in good faith any order I may receive from those in authority over me."

Speculators seeking profit from indirect trade with the enemy found no favor at his hands, but were persistently excluded from his lines. It is related that he once even kicked out of his tent one of this class who had the audacity to attempt to bribe him by the offer of a share of the profits of such illicit trade. This scrupulous integrity and devotion to the cause undoubtedly made him enemies, who disparaged and calumniated him; but it proved him all the more worthy of the love and respect of the people, and stamped him as an incorruptible patriot, to whom the highest trusts may be safely committed.

Grant was in truth the legitimate and complete product of the war, and after his triumph at Vicksburg began to be regarded as the man for the crisis. Hitherto the country had looked in vain for the great leader who should conduct to victory the grand army of men and the grand power of ideas furnished by the loyal North. One more campaign, another growth of power, another manifestation of military genius, another victory, and the government and people alike were ready to hail Ulysses S. Grant as the great captain raised up by Providence to be the deliverer of his country.

After the capture of Vicksburg, and the complete accomplishment of the purpose of the campaign, Grant suggested to the government an expedition against Mobile. He desired that his success should be promptly followed up by vigorous movements which should weaken and dispirit the rebels, and he considered Mobile as the next most important point of attack in the south-west, and at that time not very difficult to capture. His suggestions were no longer treated with contempt or indifference by Halleck, who joined him in wishing he had a sufficient force at his disposal to accomplish the purpose. But at this time England and France were meddling in the affairs of Mexico, and France was especially forward not only in crushing out Mexican republicanism, but in its propositions to mediate, or rather to interfere, in the contest between the government and the rebels. It was therefore deemed of much political importance that a strong United States force should occupy the line of the Rio Grande, to check any hostile movement which France, under false pretences, might make into United States territory. This required the forces which would have been used against Mobile, and for these reasons Grant was obliged to abandon a movement which he believed desirable, and which under his direction would probably have met with early success. But he was called to take command of more important operations, and to win the more splendid victory at Chattanooga.

Having sent many of the troops with which he was temporarily reënforced back to their several departments, and having despatched others to reënforce Banks, Grant went to New Orleans to confer with the latter general. While in that city he was thrown from his horse at a review and severely injured. For a long time he was helpless; but he continued to direct the operations and movements of his command. Before he had recovered, he received urgent despatches from Halleck to send reënforcements to Rosecrans, who was at Chattanooga confronted by Bragg. The despatches to Grant were unaccountably delayed; but as soon as received, with his usual promptness he hurried forward the reënforcements under Sherman. But in the mean time Rosecrans had not proved equal to the task confided to him, and having suffered a severe repulse at Chickamauga, was shut up in Chattanooga, short of supplies and closely besieged. The government then determined to unite all the departments between the Alleghanies and the Mississippi in one grand division, as Grant had, many months before, suggested, though he had then stated that he did not desire the command. Now, as the most successful and distinguished general in the army, he was naturally selected for this new and extensive command.

On his way up the Mississippi he received a despatch ordering him, as soon as he was able to take the field, to go to Cairo with his staff. Though yet very weak, he arrived at Cairo on the 16th of October, and immediately reported that he was ready for duty. He was at once ordered to Louisville, where he met the Secretary of War, Mr. Stanton, who brought from Washington the orders creating the new department and appointing Grant to the command. The secretary also bore other orders, which gave the general full power over all the troops in his department, with authority to conduct the campaign according to his own plans. The whole proceeding showed how much confidence the government reposed in Grant, and how much they expected of his military capacity.

There were already rumors, unfounded, however, that Rosecrans was preparing to evacuate Chattanooga, a position of the utmost importance to hold; and it was feared, from the posture of affairs, that, if not abandoned, it would be captured, and thus a still greater disaster would follow the repulse at Chickamauga. Grant, therefore, at the desire of the government, at once assumed the command and sent forward orders, by telegraph, to prevent the deprecated movement, and to relieve Rosecrans.

There was need of prompt action. Rosecrans's army was closely besieged, and Bragg felt confident that he could soon starve him out and compel a surrender.

The whole force was on half rations, and had scarcely ammunition enough for a single battle. Three thousand wounded soldiers lay in the camps, suffering and dying for the want of medical supplies. Ten thousand horses and mules had died for want of forage; and even had a retreat been contemplated, all artillery and baggage must be abandoned. From their elevated position on Lookout Mountain and Missionary Ridge the enemy was throwing shells into the town and the Union camps. The rebel forces, greatly increased and holding strong and commanding positions, were confident that they would soon possess and maintain this important strategic point, while the Union troops were daily becoming weaker and more dispirited.

Such was the condition of affairs when Grant assumed command. Besides the reënforcements which he had already ordered forward under Sherman, other troops were placed at his disposal, including the eleventh and twelfth corps from the army of the Potomac, under the command of General Hooker, and he was assured of the fullest support by the government. Although still lame and weak, Grant entered at once into the conduct of the campaign with his usual energy. He sent forward orders to hold Chattanooga at all hazards till he arrived, gave directions for Burnside's operations at Knoxville, prescribed the movements of reënforcements, ordered forward fresh provisions and medical supplies, studied the whole field, mastered its difficulties, and laid his plans. He hastened to Chattanooga as soon as possible over the precipitous mountain roads, which were rendered almost impassable by the heavy rains, but by which alone he could reach that place. He moved with a small party on horseback, and in his weak physical condition only his strong will carried him through the difficult and dangerous journey. Often the entire party were obliged to dismount in order to pass some point of extreme difficulty and danger, and then Grant, unable to walk, was carried in the arms of soldiers. But his resolution carried him through, his mind all the time occupied with the great work before him, and framing orders and despatches to be sent to every part of his wide command and to the government, which was anxiously awaiting his action.

Grant's command extended a thousand miles, and comprised three armies, numbering about two hundred thousand men. The command was more extensive than that of any other general during the war; the operations of greater magnitude, the positions and the interests at stake more important, than had yet been intrusted to one man. And the condition of the army at Chattanooga, and the urgent necessity of the speediest action, made the command still more responsible and difficult. But Grant, in spite of his physical condition, which was but slowly improving, devoted himself to his great responsibility with the most untiring energy, and the most patient attention to all the countless details of opening communications, providing supplies, forwarding troops, watching the enemy, foiling his movements, and planning defence or attack. Every movement was made by his orders; his care of every department and of every position was wonderful, and his letters, orders, and despatches, sent daily, and almost hourly, to some part of his command or to

Washington, testify not only to the amount of his labors, but to his comprehensive generalship, his fidelity to every duty, and a remarkable administrative power, which qualifies him for the highest civil as well as military position. And all was done with his characteristic quiet and self-reliance, without haste or impatience, and without ostentation.

In five days after Grant's arrival at Chattanooga, communication with Nashville was opened, by dint of energy, skilful movements, and some sharp fighting, and supplies were brought in abundance to the army, which had been living on half rations. The soldiers thus relieved, regained their spirit and enthusiasm, and hailed Grant as a leader whom they were proud to serve under. With wondrous energy, aided by his able subordinates, Thomas and Hooker, he had changed the aspect of affairs, loosened the clutch of the enemy, brought up supplies, and secured the safety of Chattanooga. And this, so promptly done, was an augury of future movements and future success, by which the defeat at Chickamauga should be avenged.

The first and most important operation, the relief and safety of the army at Chattanooga, had been accomplished, but it must be followed promptly with a similar service for Burnside's army in East Tennessee. To this Grant also gave his personal attention, his first measure being to provide supplies for Burnside in his distant and not easily accessible position. This was followed by still more important measures, contemplating the relief of Burnside's army from the superior forces of the enemy. As soon as Bragg found himself foiled at Chattanooga, he sent Longstreet, with a large force, to drive Burnside from East Tennessee. The government was exceedingly anxious to hold this section of country, not only on account of its strategic importance, but for the sake of the loyal inhabitants who had suffered the malignant persecution of the rebels. Grant was informed of the importance attached to this by the government, and appreciated the urgency of the case. But it was impossible to reënforce Burnside, for the latter had no supplies for additional troops, and there was no way of sending supplies; while to weaken the forces at Chattanooga would invite an attack on that place by Bragg's strong army. Grant therefore determined that the only way in which he could relieve Burnside was to attack the rebels before Chattanooga, and compel Longstreet to abandon his movement. For this purpose he was most anxious for the arrival of Sherman, without whose forces such an attack could not be made. But Sherman encountered many difficulties in moving his forces hundreds of miles through the enemy's country, and Grant was for once impatient, not at Sherman's delay, for he knew that was unavoidable, but lest he might be too late, and Burnside be captured or driven from East Tennessee. He urged the latter to maintain himself as long as possible, promising soon to relieve him by a movement at Chattanooga; and as Sherman's forces drew near, he several times issued orders for an attack, but was compelled to countermand them, for the very elements seemed to conspire to retard the movement of Sherman's column.

But at last the wished-for troops arrived, weary with their long and difficult march, but having all the toughness and discipline of veterans, and the confidence and ardor of victors. By skilful movements, concealed from the enemy, Sherman's army was moved through Chattanooga and across the river to confront the rebel right. The rapidity and energy with which this movement was made, involving the constructiou of bridges and transportation of troops, artillery, and supplies, were worthy of the army which, under the prompt, vigorous, and persistent lead of Grant, had made the brilliant campaign of Vicksburg. Contrast the movements of this army, not only in that arduous campaign under Grant, but in its long and difficult march under Sherman from Memphis to Chattanooga, through swamps, across rivers, over mountains, fighting and skirmishing, with the slow progress of the army of the Potomac under McClellan up the Peninsula, where there were no serious obstacles! But there was a new order of things in the army now, and especially at the west; and Hooker, who had chafed at the delays and want of vigor in the Peninsular campaign, at Chattanooga found a general who gave him all he wanted to do, expected him to surmount stupendous difficulties and fight the enemy at the same time, and who would not pause when the golden moment for decisive action came, and say, 'This is all that was intended for the day.'

The battle of Chattanooga was one of the most remarkable in the war, and indeed one of the most notable in modern history. Notwithstanding the great advantage of position the enemy enjoyed, and the difficult character of the ground, Grant so laid his plans, and they were so carried out by the skill of his subordinates and the gallantry of their troops, that the rebel forces were compelled to move as he desired, and if he had given the orders himself, their movements could not have been more consonant with his purpose. It is not necessary to give the details of the operations, or even to attempt a sketch of the brilliant movements, the gallant deeds, the splendid success of the Union army. The reader knows the story well, — how Hooker on the right, climbing the precipitous sides of Lookout Mountain, drove the enemy from point to point, from redan and rifle-pit, over cliff and boulder, till, fighting above the clouds, he planted the Stars and Stripes on the summit of the rugged mountain, and rolled back the rebel flank defeated; how Sherman on the left stormed with such energy the rebel right on Missionary Ridge, that Bragg was forced to send column after column from his centre to maintain his ground and protect his rear and stores; how, when the rebel centre was thus weakened, as by the very orders of Grant, he gave the word for the assault, and the gallant army of the Cumberland swept with irresistible force across the plain and up the steep and rugged hill, and fighting stubbornly against stubborn resistance, broke through the centre and planted their colors all along the ridge; how thus the victory began, and then the long line of Union troops with triumphant shouts pressed upon their dispirited foes, until Bragg's whole army was routed and flying before the victorious national arms. But it was no brief conflict or easily won success, for the battle lasted three days, and the victory was won only by skill, gallantry, persistency, and a heavy cost of life.

No battle of equal magnitude was ever fought more directly under the orders of the commanding general. Grant's plans were complete and well-digested, and his orders to his subordinates were clear and explicit, looking to one result, but providing for emergencies. Those orders were carried out with precision and alacrity by his able subordinates, not only because Grant was their superior officer, but because they had entire confidence in his ability. On the second, and decisive day of the battle, the general established his headquarters with Thomas, on Orchard Knoll, from which the rebels had been driven the preceding day. It was well to the front, and thus he had a full view of the whole field of operations, from Lookout Mountain on the right, down whose sides Hooker was driving the rebel left, to the extreme of Missionary Ridge on the left, where Sherman was making his vigorous assault on the strong and obstinately defended positions of the rebel right. In his front lay Thomas's army of the Cumberland, waiting for the important crisis when they should be allowed to join in the conflict, and avenge their defeat at Chickamauga.

Smoking his cigar, Grant quietly but keenly watched the tide of battle, waiting for Hooker to get into the designated position, when he might order the attack on the centre. Sherman was having a difficult task, for Bragg, regarding his right as the key to his position, or believing that to be the main attack of the Union army, concentrated heavy forces there. Seeing Sherman had paused, Grant ordered another division to his support. The movement was seen by the enemy, and it had the effect desired by Grant. A strong column was moved from the rebel centre to their right, and Grant, perceiving the opportunity for which he laid his plans, without waiting longer for Hooker, ordered the assault on the enemy's weakened centre. The troops eagerly obeyed the order, and advanced in splendid style towards the enemy's lines, utterly regardless of the heavy artillery fire which was poured into them. Without firing a gun, they charged with glistening bayonets through the enemy's first line, completely overwhelming it by their irresistible advance. Then they began to climb the steep and rugged sides of the ridge, met by a stout resistance, but steadily advancing their colors, struggling up the difficult ascent, and fighting with untiring energy and bravery.

While Grant and Thomas anxiously watched the progress of this assault, a portion of the line seemed to halt half way up the ridge, as if the troops there had met with an overpowering resistance, and the numbers of wounded men who straggled down the hill gave the appearance of a repulse. Thomas, though usually cool and collected in battle, was keenly alive to the importance of success at this crisis, and said, with much feeling and some hesitation as he watched, —

"General, I'm afraid they won't get up."

But Grant, watching more narrowly for a few minutes, saw that the colors still advanced, though slowly, and knowing that the troops must be fatigued by the extraordinary exertions of their rapid charge, but still having full confidence in them and in the success of his plans, he replied in his usual quiet manner, still smoking his cigar, —

"O, give 'em time, general; they'll do it."

And they did it. Mounting persistently up the steep ascent, they at last reached the summit, and drove the rebel centre in disorder from the field, capturing artillery and many prisoners. But as the brave troops reached the summit, Grant and Thomas mounted their horses and rode forward to the front. When they reached the ridge, the victory had been achieved, and the soldiers, wild with joy, greeted their commanders with enthusiastic cheers. Crowding around Grant, they grasped his hand and embraced his legs, and caressed his horse, till he was compelled to order them away. His eye was still upon the field, and he saw that some of the rebel troops which had gone to resist Sherman were turning to attack the victors at the centre. The "boys in blue" were in disorder from very joy for their victory, and there was danger that they would not soon enough rally to resist the threatened attack. Seeing this, Grant ordered up a brigade yet fresh and under discipline, and this being placed in position, the others also formed. The enemy, instead of attacking, retreated. The rebel left as well as centre had been utterly routed, nearly their whole force was flying panic-stricken, and the brilliant victory was won.

But Grant was not one to sit down and exult over what he had done while there was anything more to do. He immediately ordered pursuit, and himself followed to direct it. Bragg's defeated army retreated in all haste, or rather fled, much of it utterly demoralized, though a portion, at one or two points, offered a vigorous resistance to the pursuers. The roads were strown with artillery and small arms, ammunition and baggage, and the wounded and stragglers were found in large numbers. No such utter defeat had been inflicted upon the rebel forces in any great battle of the war. At Antietam and Gettysburg the enemy had been worsted with heavy loss, and, his invasion thoroughly checked, he had retired suddenly, but in order, and choosing his own time. At Chattanooga the rebel army had been driven from a position of great natural strength, fortified with skill and defended with stubbornness, and, routed and demoralized, it had been chased back with heavy losses into the heart of the rebel Confederacy.

As soon as the pursuit terminated on the day following the victory, Grant sent Sherman to East Tennessee to the relief of Burnside, who had already repulsed Longstreet in a desperate assault at Knoxville. The approach of Sherman's forces caused Longstreet to retire, and Knoxville was left secure.

"Considering the strength of the rebel position," says General Halleck, "and the difficulty of storming his intrenchments, the battle of Chattanooga must be regarded as one of the most remarkable in history." And such is the testimony of other experienced and scientific soldiers at home and abroad. Without forgetting the gallant services of the officers and soldiers under him, the great glory of that splendid victory must be awarded to Grant, who came, fed, strengthened, and encouraged a besieged and dispirited army, and marshalled it for battle. To him the untiring director of all the operations, the vigorous mover and efficient feeder of troops, the able strategist and skilful tactician, the persistent and confident commander, the country is indebted for that signal success which was the forerunner of other victories, and one of the severest blows to the rebel Confederacy.

The country recognized its obligations, and everywhere among the gallant soldiers and the loyal people the name of Grant was hailed with grateful joy. President Lincoln promptly sent him a telegram, in which he said, "I wish to tender you, and all under your command, my more than thanks, my profoundest gratitude, for the skill, courage, and perseverance with which you and they, over so great difficulties, have effected that important object. God bless you all." Congress unanimously voted a resolution of thanks, and ordered a gold medal, commemorating the victory, to be presented to Grant by the President, "in the name of the people of the United States of America."

But amid all the praise and admiration with which he was everywhere received by citizens and soldiers, and all the honors awarded by the government, he was never elated, and he assumed no superiority, but was always the same simple, honest, and unpretending man that he had been before he became the ablest and most successful general of his time, — a genuine republican soldier.

## CHAPTER VII.

Grant's Activity, Policy, and Plans. — The Necessity for placing the Armies under one efficient Commander. — The Man for the Place, and the Place for the Man. — Appointed Lieutenant General. — The Honor and the Responsibility. — Unsought by Grant. — All his Promotions made without his Knowledge. — Called to Washington. — Cordial Relations with Sherman and McPherson. — No Jealousy among his Subordinates. — Modest Appearance at Washington. — Dislikes the "Show Business." — Presentation of his Commission. — President Lincoln's Address and Grant's Reply. — A Commission worthily bestowed. — Grand Reviews and Military Balls in McClellan's Time. — Disapproved by the Lieutenant General. — He disappoints the Ladies. — Reviews for Utility, not Show. — His Opinion of the Army of the Potomac. — Customs and Abuses reformed. — Reduction of Baggage. — Grant's Baggage in the Vicksburg Campaign. — Quiet and unostentatious Method of reforming Abuses. — Temporary Return to the West. — His first Orders as Lieutenant General. — Headquarters in the Field. — With the Army of the Potomac. — Confidence of the loyal People. — Entire Trust of the Government. — Relations between President Lincoln and Grant. — Their Letters on the Eve of the great Campaign.

AFTER the victory at Chattanooga, Grant personally inspected every part of this extensive department, his purpose being so to dispose his troops that he might assume the offensive in the spring, still making the rebel armies his objective. He sent an expedition, under Sherman, from Vicksburg into the interior of Mississippi, for the purpose of "cleaning out" the rebel forces in that state, and so destroying communications and supplies that large armies could not easily move there; and he kept all his forces well in advance, in order that he and not the rebels might take the initiative in the next campaign. That was Grant's policy always, to assume the offensive; to seek out the enemy, and strike him boldly and vigorously. At this time, too, he projected, as his next campaign, an advance from Chattanooga to Atlanta, and thence, possibly, to Mobile. And from this plan resulted Sherman's brilliant movements to Atlanta, and his grand march to the sea.

But Grant's plans for his own operations in the next campaign were destined to be considerably modified. The government and the people had long felt that in order to secure unity of purpose in the conduct of the campaigns, east and west, and an efficient coöperation between the several Union armies, it was important to have all the forces under the command of one active and able general. The generals-in-chief had thus far been unable to secure such unity of purpose and co-operation, and the country had looked anxiously for the "coming man" who should achieve what the loyal masses resolved upon. But now events pointed unmistakably to the man who was qualified, if any in the army was, for this high command. Donelson, Shiloh, Vicksburg, and Chattanooga pointed to Grant as the most successful general, while all the movements in his campaigns were seen to be the most prompt, vigorous, and well sustained in the whole progress of the war. Moreover, he was always ready to conform to the policy of the government, and without question to support it earnestly, and to secure its support for others.

He had felt no petty jealousies, and he had inspired none in others, and at this time was the one who, of all others, could be promoted to the highest command without causing heart-burnings and insubordination, which would have been dangerous to the efficiency of the army.

The man for the place having thus unmistakably appeared, a measure which had been for some time under consideration in Congress was adopted. The grade of Lieutenant General, which had been first created for Washington, and was conferred by brevet on Scott alone, was revived with great unanimity, and the President was authorized to appoint, with the advice and consent of the Senate, from among those officers most distinguished for courage, skill, and ability, a commander, "who, being commissioned as lieutenant general, shall be authorized, under the direction of the President, to command the armies of the United States." President Lincoln approved the bill on the 1st of March, 1864, and on the same day nominated Major General Ulysses S. Grant as Lieutenant General. The Senate promptly confirmed the nomination, and thus Grant was promoted to the highest military rank then recognized by law, and to the command of all the armies engaged in crushing the gigantic rebellion.

Such honor had been fully bestowed upon but one man before, and that one Washington; such power and responsibilities had been intrusted to no one. But honors and responsibilities came to Grant unsought, and were accepted with becoming modesty and with hopeful self-reliance, his only aim being to do his duty and serve his country. His position at this time is best described by Hon. E. B. Washburne, of Illinois, a friend who had come to know him well and to fully appreciate him, and who, in a speech in Congress, said, "No man, with his consent, has ever mentioned Grant's name in connection with any position. I say what I know to be true, when I allege that every promotion he has received since he first entered the service to put down this rebellion, was moved without his knowledge or consent. And in regard to this very matter of lieutenant general, after the bill was introduced and his name mentioned in connection therewith, he wrote to me, and admonished me that he had been highly honored by the government, and did not ask or deserve anything more in the shape of honors or promotion; and that a success over the enemy was what he craved above anything else."

On the 3d of March he was summoned to Washington; and though he obeyed the order with alacrity, as he did all orders from the government, it was without ostentation or exultation, but with a just sense of the heavy responsibilities which were about to be imposed upon him. His modesty and his justice to the merits of his subordinates are illustrated by a friendly letter, which he wrote at this time to Sherman and McPherson, in which he acknowledged, with perhaps too little credit to himself, how much of his success was due to the energy and skill of his subordinates, and especially to those distinguished officers. The cordial relations and friendship which existed between Grant and his able lieutenants was remarkable. They not only felt no jealousy, but they heartily rejoiced at his promotion. Nor was this feeling confined to the officers who had served under him. General Halleck, whom by his new appointment he superseded, and who was at first slow to acknowledge Grant's merits, sincerely congratulated him on this recognition of his distinguished and meritorious services. General Meade, also, and other prominent officers of the eastern army, recognized his ability, and entertained nothing but respect for the man who *by his merits alone* had attained to such distinguished honor, and who so modestly wore it.

Grant arrived at Washington on the 8th of March, accompanied by two or three members of his staff and his eldest son, and almost an entire stranger in the city. Quietly entering his name on the register at Willard's Hotel, he modestly took his place among strangers at the table, with his boy, evidently seeking to avoid rather than to court public recognition. The crowd of guests did not see in the unassuming officer, who had come without any heralding, the man who had just been appointed to the highest military rank. But he was at last recognized by one gentleman, and the news passing rapidly through the company, he was greeted with enthusiastic cheers. That evening he attended the President's levee, and there he was the object of more striking demonstrations of enthusiasm, in which the President himself heartily joined. The victorious general who captured Donelson, defeated the rebels at Shiloh, made the brilliant and successful campaign of Vicksburg, and drove Bragg's legions from before Chattanooga, could not escape the grateful plaudits of the people, nor, as the newly-appointed Lieutenant General, fail to receive the most cordial tokens of the confidence and hopes which he inspired.

Deeply impressed by these demonstrations, and grateful for the manifestations of respect and confidence so fully and heartily bestowed, Grant was nevertheless unused to such things, and had a decided aversion to being lionized. As he left the White House he said to a friend, —

"I hope to get away from Washington as soon as possible, for *I am tired of the show business* already."

The next day, March 9th, a more impressive scene took place in the Cabinet Chamber of the White House, when President Lincoln formally presented to Grant his commission as Lieutenant General. The presentation took place in presence of the members of the Cabinet, General Halleck, two members of General Grant's staff, his son, Hon. Owen Lovejoy, and one or two others who had been invited to be present. After Grant had been introduced to the members of the Cabinet, President Lincoln addressed him as follows:

"General Grant, the nation's appreciation of what you have done, and its reliance upon you for what remains to be done in the existing great struggle, are now presented with this commission, constituting you Lieutenant General in the army of the United States. With this high honor devolves upon you, also, a corresponding responsibility. As the country herein trusts you, so, under God, it will sustain you. I scarcely need add that, with what I here speak for the nation, goes my own hearty personal concurrence."

Receiving the commission, General Grant replied, —

"Mr. President, I accept the commission, with gratitude for the high honor conferred. With the aid of the noble armies that have fought in so many fields for our common country, it will be my earnest endeavor not to disappoint your expectations. I feel the full weight of the responsibilities now devolving on me; and I know that if they are met, it will be due to those armies, and, above all, to the favor of that Providence which leads both nations and men."

Such was the spirit with which this most important commission was given and received — confidence and hope on the one side, patriotism and modest devotion to duty on the other. And never was such a commission, involving so much the honor, safety, and integrity of the nation, more worthily bestowed. For in Grant the country had not only an officer whose ability had been fully proved in long campaigns and on great battle-fields, but one who inspired the truest enthusiasm and confidence of the soldier and the harmony and respect of his subordinate officers, and who himself manifested, without ambition or selfishness, a thorough respect for and deference to the wishes and commands of his superior, the President, and his sympathy with the war policy of his government.

Washington, as the capital of the nation, is of course a place famous for fêtes, balls, and all sorts of gay festivities. The war had made little difference in this respect, except that the southern aristocracy did not now rule society there. While McClellan commanded, and the army of the Potomac was waiting before Washington, there had been "grand reviews," at which the commanding general was "attended by a brilliant staff," and all the beauty and fashion of the city came out to see and to be entertained at his headquarters, and those of subordinate generals. Pleasant times those for young officers, and equally agreeable to the gay belles who admired such brave cavaliers. Balls in camp followed the grand reviews, and of course gallant officers exerted themselves to make everything charming for their fair guests and distinguished visitors. Pleasure-seeking ladies voted these festivities delightful; and as the gay scenes hid from their view the horrors and sorrows of war, — the battle-field, the hospital, the desolated home, — they were ever ready to contribute their part to such agreeable entertain ments. The fashion set in McClellan's time had been duly observed when an opportunity offered.

The appointment of Grant to a superior rank, and his accession to the command of all the armies, seemed to some of the thoughtless a rare opportunity for the revival of the "grand reviews," and the gay ball to follow it. The project was buzzed about with approbation at one of the receptions of some official host, at which Grant was present, and a bevy of ladies gathered about him to propose it. They expatiated on the enjoyments of such occasions in the past, and with all their witchery begged him to have another grand review, and allow them to arrange for another military ball to follow it. Grant listened with the quiet politeness which he always shows to ladies, smiling at their eagerness, and putting a few questions relative to former festivities, and the assailants thought they were about to carry the fortress, to secure an "unconditional surrender" to their demands and their plans. But the new Lieutenant General dashed their hopes by saying, —

"Ladies, please stop the agitation of this subject at once, for if another ball is attempted in the army of the

Potomac, I shall feel called upon to forbid it by a special order. I appeal to you if this is a time for feasting and dancing among officers of the army, when the stern duties of war are before them? Or are they becoming, when our country is in danger, and so many sick and wounded soldiers fill our hospitals?"

There was no help for it, and the ladies gracefully surrendered to the quiet and sensible determination of the new Lieutenant General, and the young officers of the army of the Potomac soon forgot their dreams of such gayeties in earnest preparation for the realities of war.

Reviews, however, were had, not that the Lieutenant General might display a brilliant staff either to spectators or the army, nor that he might please the soldiers by complimentary remarks or grandiloquent addresses, but that he might see of what material this noble army of the Potomac was composed, and what was its equipment and discipline. After one of these reviews he was one day asked what he thought of the *personnel* of the army, and replied, —

"This is a very fine army, and these men, I am told, have fought with great bravery. But I think," he added, after a pause, "the army of the Potomac has *never fought its battles through*."

Whether the opinion was entirely just or not, it illustrated Grant's own character for indomitable energy and persistency, and manifested also his faith in that army which, under his direction, was to display his characteristics, and fight its battles *through* to the final victory.

The army of the Potomac had been, through nearly all its existence, so near to the national capital, and within such easy communication with the great cities and the manufacturing States of the Atlantic coast, that it was supplied with some comforts and luxuries which were not enjoyed by the western armies. The nature of its campaigns, too, and frequent communication with Washington, had gradually introduced customs which were unknown in western campaigns. The amount of officers' baggage, especially during the months of comparative inactivity, had materially increased, and was much larger than that carried in the campaigns at the west. In the Vicksburg campaign Grant had ordered the amount of baggage, both of officers and regiments, to be reduced to the smallest possible amount, and it was facetiously said that all that the general allowed himself was "a pocket-comb, a tooth-brush, and a brier-wood pipe."

Another custom had grown up at the east for officers to use ambulances, and even more luxurious carriages, for transportation from one point to another, and many horses and vehicles were thus used without any legitimate authority, sometimes much to the dissatisfaction of the soldiers, who were precluded from such privileges, and not much to the advantage of the officers.

Sutlers, too, and other camp followers, were numerous, making discipline more lax, and interfering with the efficiency of the army in active service.

When Grant assumed the direction of the movements of the army, his first action was quietly to reform these abuses, to reduce the quantity of baggage allowed to officers and regiments, to prohibit the use of ambulances and carriages by officers on ordinary occasions, and to drive out a large number of sutlers and camp followers. These measures were, to the credit of officers and men, acquiesced in without much complaint, and the army was made more ready for the campaign which was to follow. They were carried out, too, by Grant, in his usual quiet way, with a tact and absence of all parade, or public condemnation, which avoided offence, and secured willing coöperation.

When Grant was summoned to Washington to be invested with the command of all the armies of the United States, he expected soon to return to the west, and resume command of the forces which had already achieved such victories under him. But after a council of war had been held at the capital, and Grant had matured his general plans of the campaigns for all the armies, he determined to remain at the east. As commander-in-chief he might with propriety have established his headquarters at Washington, and directed the various operations from that place. But he felt out of his element in Washington, and preferred to be in the field, directing in person the active operations of one army, while he more indirectly ordered the movements of the others. The campaign in Virginia, where the opposing armies had been so long contending without decisive results, promised to be the most difficult and severe, and gave him the opportunity of rendering the greatest service to his country; and he therefore determined to take the field with the army of the Potomac, the immediate command of which was still held by General Meade. Going west for a short time, to consult with General Sherman, and give directions concerning the campaign there, he issued his first orders, assuming command of all the armies, at Nashville, on the 17th of March. In those orders he announced, "My headquarters will be in the field, and until further orders, will be with the army of the Potomac."

This announcement was highly gratifying to the army of the Potomac and to the loyal people, whose confidence in Grant was such that they believed the brave soldiers of that noble but too often unfortunate army, under his able and persistent lead, would achieve a signal success, which should not only foil an invasion of the north by the rebels, but ultimately defeat them utterly and forever.

General Grant, indeed, entered upon his heavy responsibilities and duties under all the advantages of entire trust on the part of the government and a majority of the people, and their determination to sustain him to the extent of their power. Every exertion was made to strengthen the armies, and to give effect to all the measures which he proposed. The nature of his relations with his only superior officer, the President, is shown by the following correspondence, which took place on the eve of the great campaign against Richmond. Those cordial relations were maintained through the life of President Lincoln.

EXECUTIVE MANSION,<br>WASHINGTON, April 30, 1864.

LIEUTENANT GENERAL GRANT: Not expecting to see you before the spring campaign opens, I wish to express in this way my entire satisfaction with what you have done up to this time, so far as I understand it. The particulars of your plan I neither know nor seek to know.

You are vigilant and self-reliant, and pleased with this I wish not to obtrude any restraints or constraints upon you. While I am very anxious that any great disaster or capture of our own men may be avoided, I know that these points are less likely to escape your attention than they would be mine. If there be anything wanting which is within my power to give, do not fail to let me know it. And now, with a brave army and a just cause, may God sustain you.

Yours very truly,

A. LINCOLN.

HEADQUARTERS ARMY OF THE U. S.,
CULPEPPER C. H., VA., May 1, 1864.

MR. PRESIDENT: Your very kind letter of yesterday is just received. The confidence you express for the future, and satisfaction for the past, in my military administration, is acknowledged with pride. It shall be my earnest endeavor that you and the country shall not be disappointed. From my first entry into the volunteer service of the country to the present day, I have never had cause of complaint, and have never expressed or implied a complaint against the administration or the Secretary of War for throwing any embarrassment in the way of my vigorously prosecuting what appeared to be my duty. Indeed, since the promotion which placed me in command of all the armies, and in view of the great responsibility and importance of success, I have been astonished at the readiness with which everything asked for has been yielded without even an explanation being asked. Should my success be less than I desire and expect, the least I can say is, the fault is not with you.

Very truly your obedient servant,

U. S. GRANT, *Lieutenant General.*

# CHAPTER VIII.

Campaign against Richmond. — Grant's Vigor and his Staff. — Strategy. — Grant with the Army of the Potomac.. — His Tenacity. — No such Thing as Defeat. — His Eye always towards the Front. — He didn't believe in Disaster. — Practical Application of Science. — Use of a Rebel Shell. — Flank Movement. — "On to Richmond." — At Spottsylvania. — The famous Despatch: "I propose to fight it out on this line." — A Pause in the Fight, and efficient Work in the Rear. — Croakers' Talk of Strategy and Copperhead Abuse. — Grant's Purpose. — Hard Fighting and Strategy equally valued. — The Purpose never abandoned. — Desperate Resistance of the Enemy. — Grant's skilful Manœuvres. — His Hold on Lee. — General Butler's Movement. — Grant disappointed. — Before Petersburg. — The Rebels kept busy. — The Weldon Railroad. — Laying Plans and waiting the Developments of other Campaigns. — A new Clamor. — Sherman's brilliant Operations. — THE FINAL CAMPAIGN. — Grant the Director. — His Strategy, Manœuvres, Sagacity, and Persistency. — Flight of Jeff Davis and Retreat of Lee's Army. — Grant chooses Lee's Route. — The Pursuit. — Lee in a Strait. — Correspondence. — The Interview at Appomattox. — The Surrender and Downfall of the Rebel Confederacy. — Joy of the People. — Grant's Honors well won. — What he had done.

AS soon as the general plan of the campaign of 1864 had been determined upon by Grant, he went vigorously to work to carry it into effect. He had no taste for show, and gave no time to it. He did not believe in delay, and would not tolerate it. Ready to work himself, and capable of accomplishing a great deal of labor, he set a good example, and required it to be followed. His headquarters were always distinguished by the quiet, business-like industry of his staff and clerks. And in the selection of his staff, he chose only men of capacity for their several duties, never simply for their good looks or social position, as some officers did, nor for mere friendship. No intimation of his plans ever leaked out from his headquarters to reach alike the loyal press and the rebel commanders. The Lieutenant General kept his own counsel, except so far as it was necessary to intrust a knowledge of his purposes to his subordinates; and his staff learned reticence from his example, if not from his injunctions.

The government heartily supported the man to whom it had intrusted the whole military power. Supplies and munitions were furnished without stint, and all that Grant deemed necessary at any point was furnished as promptly as possible. The country, too, sent forward troops with unfailing zeal, and the armies were filled up to a strength they had never before reached. Two years before, after great preparation and long delay, after many grand reviews and much unpractical discipline, a commander, of whom the country unwisely expected as much as they did now of Grant, had begun the first campaign against Richmond. From the outset, he had asked for reënforcements, and the burden of all his despatches was "more troops," "more troops," or something more and different from what the government had provided or proposed, not because he had *proved* the strength of the enemy, but because he *feared* it, and was ready to magnify it. And so the very delays resulting from his dissatisfaction with what he had, and his distrust of his troops, if not of his own capacity, served to make the enemy as formidable as he had feared.

It is true that there had now been a great improvement in military affairs. The army was better organized, better equipped, and better officered, and experience had made both men and officers more efficient. But Grant, on assuming command, had made no extravagant demands, and sought no extraordinary power. Never in all his campaigns had he clamored for reënforcements. He had always taken what the government could send, and made the best possible use of them. So, as the commander of all the armies, he evinced the same spirit, trusting to the patriotism of the government and the people to furnish all that they could to accomplish the work of crushing the rebellion, and resolved to do his part by a faithful and persistent use of the means thus placed in his hands. His letter to President Lincoln, quoted in the preceding chapter, shows how he acknowledged the efforts of the government, and with what a generous spirit he recognized his own responsibility.

As Grant's strategy in his former campaigns had been simply to make the rebel armies his objective, so in his wider field he did not change it. The rebel army in Virginia was the objective of the eastern campaign, and the rebel army between Chattanooga and Atlanta was the objective of the western campaign. These two armies comprised the mass of the rebel forces, and covered the vital points of the rebel Confederacy, and they were to be the objects towards which the two great Union armies were to move; all other operations being in aid of these, to create diversions, or to hold detached rebel forces from joining the main rebel armies. Neither Richmond nor Atlanta were considered strategic points which it was important to reach and hold, but Grant's purpose was to reach and defeat the rebel armies, whether in front of those places, or wherever they might be made to give battle. In them was the strength of the rebellion, and with their defeat it would be conquered.

Grant's combined movements were made early in May, General Sherman succeeding him in the immediate command of the western army, Grant himself, as before stated, directing the campaign in Virginia, General Meade being in immediate command. Coöperating with the army of the Potomac was a force under General Butler, which moved up the James River towards Richmond, and upon the operations of which Grant relied for early success, and another under General Sigel, which moved up the Shenandoah Valley.

Though General Meade remained in immediate command of the army of the Potomac, it was unmistakably a satisfaction to the country that General Grant was present to direct the campaign and to fight the battles. The army too was inspired by his presence; for his previous success, his acknowledged ability, and his well-known perseverance, were an assurance of ultimate victory. His unassuming, quiet, self-reliant manner, and his republican simplicity, also impressed the soldiers and won their respect. For the Union army was a democratic army, and essentially Anglo-Saxon, or certainly not French enough to be long carried away by Napoleonic displays of military grandeur, high-sounding addresses, and lofty condescension, such as in its earlier days seemed to be the spirit of the head-quarters of the army of the Potomac. The soldiers had learned to judge of officers by their success, and not by brave words or brilliant promises; by their energy and activity, and not by a showy staff or excess of etiquette.

As the campaign progressed, he imparted to officers and men something of his own persistency and indomitable purpose, and thus carried them through terrible conflicts and trying emergencies, which, without his presence and direction, might have resulted in discouragement and defeat.

The advance from the Rapidan to Richmond illustrated Grant's tenacity of purpose, and the battles illustrated his skill as a tactician. They were the most obstinate contests of the war; for here was the flower of the rebel army under their ablest officers, fighting for their capital, and knowing that with their defeat the rebel Confederacy must go down in ignominy. The campaign was vital to both the contestants; for, while defeat of the rebels was the death-blow to the rebellion, a defeat of the Union army would have involved a similar fate to the western army, and could be retrieved only by still greater sacrifices of blood and treasure. Nay, defeat now involved more than this, for a disloyal peace party at the North, and foreign intervention, would have profited by such a disaster, and the rebel Confederacy would have become a recognized nation. Fortunate for the country was it that it had such a man as Grant to lead its principal armies at such a crisis, — a soldier of tried skill, of inexhaustible resources, unfaltering persistency, and who, with the confidence of a fatalist, knew no such thing as defeat.

Grant never supposed such a thing as defeat possible, though he never placed his army in a position from which his skill could not extricate it in case of necessity. His eye and his thoughts were always turned towards the front and on his own aggressive movements, and he found no time to direct them to the rear. He took care that the quartermasters, with ample supplies, should always be there, and that was the only reason for keeping his communications open, for he never thought of return.

It would have taken a terrible defeat to make Grant believe it, so strong was his faith in success. At the battle of the Wilderness, when the rebels, massing heavily against Hancock's corps, pressed it back, an aid brought word to Grant that the corps had suffered serious disaster. "I don't believe it," said the general, with something more of vehemence than usual; and he sent the aid back for further reports, which proved that the first accounts were greatly exaggerated. The nature of the country where the battle of the Wilderness was fought was such as to make it but little better than a fight in the dark. A thick, low growth of wood on a wide plain, with only moderate elevations, concealed the movements of both friend and foe, except where they were actually engaged, and it was impossible for the commanding general or his subordinates to direct the movements of the troops with the precision which had been shown at Chattanooga. Though the rebels could see no better, the ground was more familiar to them, and they had only to feel the position of an army just advancing into the Wilderness. An open country, where he could see the enemy's lines, and the advantages or disadvantages of his own position, might have enabled Grant, with his skilful manœuvres and grand tactics and tenacity, to achieve a victory on the first field, which he was determined to achieve somewhere.

The obscurity of the field, and Grant's practical mind, which in a campaign was full of resources for great occasions or small, are shown by an incident at his headquarters. A rebel shell struck quite near to himself and Meade as they were conversing together, furrowing the ground and bursting at some distance. Though the shell came unpleasantly near, Grant neither started nor spoke, but he put it to some use. Drawing from his pocket a small compass, he calculated the course of the shell, and in a few minutes he had some artillery posted to silence the rebel battery which had thrown it. The guns thus posted and pointed soon silenced the unseen battery, and Grant, inquiring the elevation of the guns, calculated the position and distance of the enemy's line, and acted promptly on the result.

Not content to fight, as it were, in the dark, where he could not strike a decisive blow, Grant had recourse to a flank movement, which, in his progress towards Richmond, soon became famous. Severing his communications at the Rapidan, he moved the army to Spottsylvania, for the purpose of placing it between Lee's army and the rebel capital, or forcing him to accept battle on a different field. Having determined upon this movement, he sent to the President the following brief despatch:—

"I am on to Richmond. All goes well."

In allusion to this despatch, the President said, with characteristic point,—

"General Grant has gone ahead, and drawn his ladder after him."

But the rebels had the advantage of interior lines, and, perceiving Grant's movement, reached Spottsylvania first. There they already had fortifications, which they promptly strengthened, and occupied a strong position. The country was more favorable for grand tactics, and Grant made some brilliant manœuvres and attacks, which forced the rebels within their strongest works. It was from this place that he sent to Washington his famous despatch, which thrilled the country with its determined spirit, and became familiar throughout the land. It simply recounted, in the briefest possible terms, what had been done, and his own determination. It contained no boast, and no extravagant promise; no call for reënforcements, and no complaint; but it showed the spirit of the great commander, and that with which he inspired the army.

IN THE FIELD, May 11, 1864.

We have now ended the sixth day of very heavy fighting. The result to this time is much in our favor.

Our losses have been heavy, as well as those of the enemy. I think the loss of the enemy must be greater.

We have taken over five thousand prisoners in battle, while he has taken from us but few, except stragglers.

*I propose to fight it out on this line if it takes all summer.*

The army of the Potomac was likely to "fight its battles through" now, if it never had before.

But the rebel position was one of great strength, and could be carried only by greatly superior numbers or at a heavy sacrifice of life; and the army, after its eight days of fighting and marching, needed rest. Grant therefore ceased to attack, and the rebels had suffered too much to assume the offensive. In this pause, all the vast work necessary for the support of a great army — the bringing up of supplies, removal of the wounded, and the arrival of reënforcements — went on with unusual celerity and success, and all the arrangements were perfected for establishing a new base when the army moved. Never before during the war had the quartermaster's department been so efficiently administered; and not a little of its promptness and efficiency were due to the direction and influence of Grant, who had already at the west proved himself the ablest of administrative officers.

During this brief delay, Grant determined upon his next move, which was another flank movement to force the rebel army back, farther from Washington, nearer to Richmond. But Lee, also, had made preparations to move; and, having still interior lines, he retired to another and stronger position between the North Anna and South Anna Rivers. Some persons, who were continually talking about "strategy," and who were, doubtless, admirers of the strategy of the first campaign against Richmond, imagined Grant was simply an obstinate fighter, and possessed no attribute of a good general. Copperhead admirers of McClellan, such as had before maligned the hero of Donelson and

Vicksburg, now called him a "butcher" who wantonly sacrificed his own men. But such malignant charges originated only with those whose sympathies were not with the Union sacrifices but with the rebel losses, and who hated Grant because he was hammering at the rebellion with the purpose of *crushing it, and not parleying with it.*

Grant's purpose was to drive the rebel army back *forever* from its threatening position too near to Washington; to fight it at all times, and in all places, when necessary; to "hammer" at it, and deal it frequent and heavy blows, from which it could not recover. But whenever his purpose could be better gained by strategy and manœuvring, he resorted to them with a skill not inferior to his persistency in fighting. So at the South Anna, without a battle, he again flanked the enemy, and forced him nearer to Richmond. Hard fighting followed, for the rebels grew more and more desperate as they were driven towards their capital, but they struggled in vain. It is true they were not beaten, though they suffered irreparable losses; but they achieved no victory, — for a victory to them was nothing less than the utter defeat of the Union army, and the abandonment of its purpose.

In the previous campaigns of these opposing armies, after a great battle, one or the other had withdrawn, — at Fredericksburg and Chancellorsville, the Union army; at Antietam and Gettysburg, the rebels. But in this campaign the rebels found a change in the tactics of the Union army. Grant massed his troops, and launched heavy columns against them, after the manner of their own ablest generals; and when his forces were checked, and the attacks failed, he did not withdraw, discouraged or disconcerted, but held on still, and, with ready resources, changed his plan, *but never abandoned his purpose.* The battles of the Wilderness, Spottsylvania, and Cold Harbor, were among the severest of the war, and the rebels fought with a desperation they had never before shown, and which they believed must triumph. But northern persistency, under the lead of Grant, was a match for southern fire and desperation. The army of the Potomac was no longer to be shaken off or compelled to retire.

It is not to be supposed that the campaign plans of even the greatest military genius can be fully carried out in their details if opposed by an enemy of even ordinary skill and bravery. Grant was contending with the most skilful generals of the rebel Confederacy, and with their strongest army of veteran soldiers, animated with the belief that they were fighting the desperate battles which must decide the fate of the rebellion. He was forced to modify or wholly change his plans, but *he never changed his purpose*, which was, sooner or later, on one field or another, to defeat and destroy Lee's army. In changing his plans, he proved his abundant and ready resources, and, trusting to his subordinates for the skilful execution of skilfully laid plans, he did not hesitate to adopt some bold manœuvres and unexpected movements. The withdrawal of the army from the closest contact with the rebels at Cold Harbor, and the flank movement made before their eyes, was a daring trial of a dangerous piece of tactics; but its boldness and admirable execution made it a complete success. It showed, in Grant, a perfect appreciation of the situation, courage, skill, resources, and tenacity of purpose. He had found Lee's army stronger than he had hoped, and he had not defeated it before it reached the defences of Richmond; but he had driven it from its fortified lines on the Rapidan back to the very streets of Richmond; had hammered it, wasted it, and dealt it heavy blows; and now, with an inflexible purpose and an unwavering confidence, he skilfully and successfully changed his base, and transferred his army to the south side of the James. But he still had his hold on Lee, *and he kept it to the end.*

A part of Grant's plan for the campaign was the movement of an army, under General Butler, up James River, to secure possession of the south bank, occupy Petersburg, and hold the rebel railroad communications with the South. He had expected important results from this expeditionary army, which was supposed to be amply sufficient to accomplish the purpose, so long as the army of the Potomac acted the vigorous part assigned it. General Butler's prompt and decisive manner of dealing with the rebels at New Orleans led Grant to hope for similar energy and success in the conduct of this movement. But, whether the failure was due to the want of military ability in Butler or his subordinates, or to the inadequacy of the forces, the movement on Petersburg failed, and Butler's army, after a short time, was besieged in its intrenchments at Bermuda Hundred, and suffered some reverses. This result, which disappointed his hopes and expectations, and doubtless led to a change of plans and a prolonged contest, confirmed Grant's prejudices against military appointments for political considerations. His experience with McClernand's inefficiency, insubordination, and conceit, led him, upon Butler's failure, to regard the latter in a similar light. Subsequent events did not increase his confidence in Butler's military capacity, and with straightforward and soldierly frankness he expressed it. Butler's irrepressible nature did not accept this kindly, and, in a war of words, noticeable only because of his prominent political position, he gave vent to his feelings. But if Butler will rest his reputation on his earlier services, and on his expedition to New Orleans, and his able and effective administration of affairs in that rebellious city, no one more than Grant will award him the fullest credit.

Finding, upon trial, that it was too late to take the strong fortifications of Petersburg by assault, Grant determined to invest them, extending his lines to the north side of the James, and gradually on the south side of Petersburg. But while he undertook the siege of the rebel stronghold, he was so constantly active that he kept Lee's army on the defensive, and prevented him from sending any very large force to create a diversion. Lee, indeed, undertook one such diversion by sending Ewell down the valley of the Shenandoah, but Grant transferred a sufficient force to meet him, and, under the gallant lead of Sheridan, Ewell and his army were utterly defeated. The ease and rapidity with which he transferred his troops — a whole corps at once— from one point to another, across the James, and from one flank to the other, illustrated not only the increased mobility of the army, but Grant's skilful direction and vigorous activity.

By persistent movements to the left, Grant seized the Weldon Railroad, an important line of communication between Richmond and the South, and held it against all the efforts of the rebels to regain it. The tenacity with which he held what he gained was illustrated at that time, as the reader may recollect, by a popular cartoon in one of the pictorial papers, in which Grant was represented as a mastiff sitting composedly before the bone of contention, and asking the canine rebels, "Why don't you come and take it?" Other advantages were gained, and cavalry raids interrupted the rebel communications, and subjected them to loss and a dearth of supplies which discouraged both army and people. But Grant was now waiting for the developments of other campaigns, laying his plans and making preparations for the final and successful operations which were to commence as soon as the proper time arrived.

During this period of comparative inactivity and absence of palpable results, the country, ignorant of what was in store, became again a little impatient. There were some who clamored for more active operations; and though the general faith in Grant was not lost, there were occasional demands that he should give place to Sherman, who appeared more active. But Grant, undisturbed by such clamors, quietly pursued his way, conscious that he was faithfully serving his country, and confident that his plans, embracing the movements of all the armies, would result in that great and final success which the country desired.

In the mean time Sherman had made his brilliant and successful campaign to Atlanta, and by strategy and hard fighting had driven Johnston *into* that place to be deprived of his command. By strategy he had forced Hood, Johnston's successor, *out* of Atlanta, and captured the town. Then sending Thomas with sufficient force back to Nashville to punish the rashness of Hood, he had cut loose from his base, and made his great march from Atlanta to the sea; and, under orders from Grant, was on his more difficult but no less successful march through the Carolinas, where Johnston, restored to command by the despair of the rebel leaders, was vainly preparing to resist him. Spring opened, and the auspicious moment for which Grant had anxiously waited was at hand. It was not suffered to pass. The army was in excellent condition and spirits, and with characteristic promptness and energy the Lieutenant General commenced his final and most brilliant campaign.

It is not necessary to go at all into the details of that memorable campaign, the splendid achievements and glorious results of which are fresh in the reader's mind. In conception, plan, and execution, it was Grant's — the result of no council of war, of no important suggestions from other officers or the government. His strategy had brought Sherman's grand army from Savannah into North Carolina almost within reach, and had moved another large force under Hancock up the Valley of the Shenandoah and towards Lynchburg, while the army of the James threatened Richmond on the south-east, and the army of the Potomac, south of Petersburg, and between Lee and Johnston, only waited for his orders to commence the battle, or series of battles, which should overthrow the hard-pressed rebel Confederacy. His manœuvres secured the chief battle-field of his own selection. His orders massed the troops where he wanted to strike the heaviest blows. His sagacity selected the gallant Sheridan to lead the boldest movements and the hardest fighting. His keen vision saw the key to the rebel position at Five Forks, and his persistency pressed his heavy columns upon it till it was carried, and Lee sent his message of dismay to the trembling traitors at Richmond. His strategy had practically surrounded the rebel armies, and his tactics forced Lee to retreat by a line north of the Appomattox, on a route chosen by himself.

Jeff Davis and his confederate traitors of the rebel government fled precipitately from Richmond, and Lee's army evacuated that city and Petersburg, utterly defeated and demoralized. Retreating by the route which Grant had forced them to take, the rebels were promptly and vigorously pursued by a shorter road, harassed and hurried by the Union cavalry. Every skirmish resulted in their defeat, and the roads were strown with the evidences of their demoralization. Numerous guns and prisoners were captured, and the army which had so long resisted the national authority was rapidly diminishing by the desertion of the disheartened men. Not only was it pursued by the victorious army of the Potomac, but by Grant's strategy at Lynchburg, whither it was retreating, it was confronted by Hancock's forces from the Shenandoah Valley, and Stoneman's strong cavalry force was approaching from the west.

While the pursuit was still in progress, Grant,

anxious to avoid the further effusion of blood, sent to Lee the following communication: —

APRIL 7, 1865.

GENERAL: The result of the last week must convince you of the hopelessness of further resistance on the part of the army of northern Virginia in this struggle. I feel that it is so, and regard it as my duty to shift from myself the responsibility of any further effusion of blood by asking of you the surrender of that portion of the Confederate States army known as the army of northern Virginia.

U. S. GRANT, *Lieutenant General.*

To this Lee replied that he did not entertain Grant's opinion of the hopelessness of further resistance, but asked what terms would be offered. Grant promptly and generously responded: —

APRIL 8, 1865.

GENERAL: Your note of last evening, in reply to mine of same date, asking the conditions on which I will accept the surrender of the army of northern Virginia, is just received. In reply, I would say that *peace* being my great desire, there is but one condition I would insist upon, namely, that the men and officers surrendered shall be disqualified for taking up arms again against the government of the United States until properly exchanged. I will meet you, or will designate officers to meet any officers you may name for the same purpose, at any point agreeable to you, for the purpose of arranging definitely the terms upon which the surrender of the army of northern Virginia will be received.

U. S. GRANT, *Lieutenant General.*

But Lee was disposed to quibble, and desired to make terms for the whole Confederacy. He said he did not propose to surrender, but wished to know whether Grant's proposals would lead to peace, and to that end he proposed a meeting. Grant, however, true to his soldierly instincts, would assume no responsibility which did not belong to him as a military commander fighting the armed forces of the rebellion. He knew that with the government and not with him rested the authority and the duty of settling the final terms of peace and reconstruction, and he had already, on a former occasion, when requested by Lee, refused to assume any such authority to enter into a convention with the rebel government for the suspension of hostilities. He would only consent to the surrender of Lee's army upon terms which were liberal enough for the bravest foe, and which he wisely believed would terminate the great struggle. He therefore declined to meet Lee to discuss the terms of peace.

Lee soon found that his case was more hopeless than he had been disposed to admit, and was forced to ask an interview to arrange the terms of surrender offered by Grant. The request was at once acceded to, and the interview took place near Appomattox Court-house, under a tree which has since been "cut into toothpicks" as memorials of that important occasion. Lee came crestfallen and humiliated, but with the bearing of a great commander, and the formal courtesy of an aristocrat; Grant came quiet and unassuming, and with a republican simplicity of manner. They had met before, but probably had never formed an acquaintance or exchanged words. When Grant, an unknown subaltern, led a gallant charge at Chepultepec, Lee was a favorite on the staff of General Scott, and he had remained there till after secession had called for the preparations of war, and then, turning traitor to the government which had educated and honored him, carried the secrets of that government to its enemies, and joined them in their infamous rebellion. The subaltern who had once received only his contemptuous notice, was now his conqueror and the greatest general of America. The one had received the just rewards of patriotism, loyalty, and faithful service; the other the humiliation, but not the punishment, of treason.

The interview was not a protracted one. While the officers who accompanied their respective chiefs mingled in conversation as pleasant as the circumstances would allow, the latter conversed apart. Lee's endeavor to secure terms which should include the rebel government, and settle the conditions of peace, was firmly resisted by Grant, and the rebel officer was compelled to accept the simple but liberal terms of surrender which were offered, or see his wasting army utterly destroyed. With a sore heart he chose to surrender, and with formal courtesies the officers parted. The terms were dictated and accepted in writing, and the surrender of that rebel army which had so long resisted the power of the nation was speedily carried into effect. With the defeat and surrender of that army, the rebel Confederacy crumbled into dust.

Thus Grant struck the final blow which *crushed the rebellion*. With what joy and exultation and thanksgiving that victory was received throughout the loyal states! Bells rang and cannon thundered the glorious news. Business, public and private, pleasure, and sorrow even, gave way to the universal jubilee. Millions shouted praises to Grant and his victorious legions, his name blazed in illuminations in honor of the Union triumph, and he was enthusiastically hailed as the second savior of his country.

And he was fully entitled to the honors and praises awarded to him by the grateful people. Not only had he achieved this decisive and crowning victory, but through the war he had struck more heavy and damaging blows than any other general in the army, and had done more than any other to weaken and subdue the rebel armies. At Donelson, at Shiloh, at Vicksburg, and at Chattanooga, he had won great victories, which thrilled the loyal people with joy, and endeared him to their hearts. At Belmont, in the Wilderness, at Spottsylvania, and at Cold Harbor, he had struck so heavily and effectively as to stagger, if not defeat, the enemy, while never, in all his conflicts, had he been driven from the field or forced to retreat. Moreover, under his direction, as commander of all the national armies, Sherman had won his victories in Georgia, made his "grand march to the sea," and moved through the Carolinas with unvaried success, to join in a final and irresistible campaign against the exhausted Confederacy; Thomas had won his glorious victory at Nashville; Canby had captured Mobile; Terry had taken Fort Fisher and Wilmington; and Sheridan had vanquished Early in the Valley of the Shenandoah. In the campaigns under his immediate command, he had captured *more than a hundred thousand prisoners*, and hundreds of cannon, while his subordinates, in the campaigns under his general direction, had taken as many more. Wherever he commanded, wherever his orders were received, wherever his influence was felt, he had organized victory, and moved on steadily to the final triumph.

## CHAPTER IX.

Sherman's Indiscretion. — His Negotiations with Johnston disapproved. — Grant sent to assume Direction of Sherman's Movements. — His Influence with Sherman, and his Friendship for him. — The most successful General of the Age. — His military Genius recognized at Home and Abroad. — Thanks and Honors. — A new Grade established to reward him. — Appointed GENERAL of the Army. — Modest Wearing of his Honors. — Manifestation of popular Admiration. — His Recognition of the Merits of his Subordinates and the Army. — No Napoleonic Airs. — Farewell Orders to the Armies. — Justice to the Soldiers of the East and of the West. — His Fidelity to his Soldiers. — Sharing their Hardships. — His Army always supplied. — His Men protected from Imposition. — The steam-boat Captain. — The Respect and Confidence of the Army.

THE surrender of Lee was soon followed by like submission of the other rebel armies. But Johnston, under instructions from the fugitive rebel government, attempted to gain from Sherman what Lee had failed to obtain from Grant, — a negotiation for the settlement of civil as well as military matters. Sherman, less prudent than Grant, and anxious to secure peace, agreed with Johnston upon terms which confessedly exceeded his authority, and which assumed to settle some political questions contrary to the principles on which the war had been necessarily conducted. More able as a soldier than he was as a politician or diplomatist, he had agreed to terms which were considered by government and people entirely inadmissible, but having no intention of transcending his powers, he sent the terms to Washington for approval.

The government was a little startled at the comprehensive character of this agreement between one of its military officers and the representative of a suppressed rebellion, and it was at once repudiated, and Sherman was ordered to resume hostilities. The disapproval was prompt and curt, and General Grant was ordered to proceed to Sherman's headquarters and direct operations against the enemy. Sherman, nervous and excitable, was indignant at the manner in which his well-disposed but mistaken measures were rejected, and he himself snubbed, and what he would have done in his anger and chagrin, had not Grant gone to him, can hardly be imagined. He was pretty sure to do something to his own injury, however; but Grant's presence saved him, and his steadfast friendship, and calm, dispassionate words, allayed the excitement and anger of the brilliant general, and repaid him for his own kindly offices when Grant, for once, — and only once in his military career, — gave way to his feelings under a keen sense of injury. The manner in which he performed the duty required of him by the government illustrated Grant's generosity towards his subordinates, by carefully keeping in Sherman's hands the fruits of his brilliant operations, and giving him the entire credit of enforcing and receiving the surrender of Johnston.

The great achievements by which he crushed the rebellion, and put an end to one of the fiercest wars of modern times, stamped Ulysses S. Grant as the most successful general of the age. His ability as a strategist and tactician, his power of combination and of execution, his talent for command, united with his energy and persistency, in a word, his military genius, could no longer be doubted, and received the encomiums, not only of a grateful people, but of able soldiers and military critics abroad. Except Napoleon, no man of recent times had achieved so many brilliant successes, or accomplished such splendid results on so extended a field.

The thanks of the government, of the states, of popular assemblies, were freely tendered to him, and he received substantial tokens of public gratitude and private appreciation. Swords and medals were voted him by states, and among the more costly gifts presented to him, by private individuals, was an elegant house in Washington, completely furnished, an admirable library, and a munificent sum of money. These gifts were thrust upon him out of honest gratitude and admiration, and were accepted with a modest dignity characteristic of the man, and becoming his position and his relations to the givers.

Subsequently, in July, 1866, upon reorganizing the army, in order to reward him by a higher honor than the service then allowed, the grade of GENERAL of the army, the highest rank yet created in the American service, was established by act of Congress, and invested with unusual powers. The rank was created expressly for the then Lieutenant General, and though President Johnson would have preferred to select another, the universal verdict of the people, and the unmistakable purpose of the act, compelled him to nominate Ulysses S. Grant. It is needless to add that the Senate promptly confirmed the nomination, and General Grant, by his own merits, and the gratitude and confidence of his country, holds a rank *from which there can be but one promotion, and that promotion will be made by the people of the United States.*

The honors bestowed upon Grant were borne with a modesty equalled only by his ability and the greatness of his achievements. They came without his seeking; they were accepted with a determination to be worthy of them. Making a private and unofficial tour to the east and west with his family in 1865, he was made aware of the gratitude and admiration of the people. He was everywhere received with the most enthusiastic demonstrations which his private mode of travelling permitted. But everywhere he was the same quiet, unostentatious, unpretending soldier that he had been when he first entered the service as colonel in 1861, ever ready to give a hearty greeting to his comrades of the army, and with republican simplicity courteous to all. His few speeches, in response to the popular demands, were brief and modest. But the people could see that with all his modesty he was self-reliant, clear-headed, brave, and firm in the discharge of his duties.

While awarding the highest meed of praise to General Grant, the country should never forget the able subordinates and the brave men to whom, with the chivalrous spirit of a true soldier, he had always attributed his successes. He assumed no Napoleonic airs, and made to them no grandiloquent and flattering speeches, but in all his reports and despatches he acknowledged their skill and bravery, and claimed for them the credit of the results. Before the grand armies were disbanded he issued the following address, which told, once for all, after all their battles were fought, and their toils ended, and the victory won, the estimation in which he, speaking for the country, held them: —

SOLDIERS OF THE ARMIES OF THE UNITED STATES: By your patriotic devotion to your country in the hour of danger and alarm, your magnificent fighting, bravery, and endurance, you have maintained the supremacy of the Union and the Constitution, overthrown all armed opposition to the enforcement of the laws and of the proclamations forever abolishing slavery, — the cause and pretext of the rebellion, — and opened the way to the rightful authorities to restore order and inaugurate peace on a permanent and enduring basis on every foot of American soil. Your marches, sieges, and battles, in distance, duration, resolution, and brilliancy of results, dim the lustre of the world's past military achievements, and will be the patriot's precedent in the defence of liberty and right in all time to come. In obedience to your country's call you left your homes and families, and volunteered in its defence. Victory has crowned your valor, and secured the purpose of your patriotic hearts; and with the gratitude of your countrymen, and the highest honors a great and free nation can accord, you will soon be permitted to return to your homes and families, conscious of having discharged the highest duty of American citizens. To achieve these glorious triumphs, and secure to yourselves, your fellow-countrymen, and posterity the blessings of free institutions, tens of thousands of your gallant comrades have fallen, and sealed the priceless legacy with their lives. The graves of these a grateful nation bedews with tears, honors their memories, and will ever cherish and support their stricken families.

U. S. GRANT, *Lieutenant General.*

So in his final report of the war he spoke of the armies of the East and of the West with a just recognition of the services and valor of each, and with a patriotism which embraces the whole country and all the loyal people. "It has been my fortune to see the armies of both the West and the East fight battles; and from what I have seen, I know there is no difference in their fighting qualities. All that it was possible for men to do in battle they have done. . . . The splendid achievements of each have nationalized our victories, removed all sectional jealousies (of which we have unfortunately experienced too much), and the cause of crimination and recrimination that might have followed had either section failed in its duty. All have a proud record, and all sections can well congratulate themselves and each other for having done their full share in restoring the supremacy of law over every foot of territory belonging to the United States. Let them hope for perpetual peace and harmony with that enemy, whose manhood, however mistaken the cause, drew forth such herculean deeds of valor."

Not only did Grant thus recognize the bravery and endurance of the men who served under him, but through the war he was true to them as to his country. He demanded of them hard service, but he was always ready to share their hardships and exposure. He counted himself as one of them. His language was, "More difficulties and privations are before us;

let us endure them manfully. Other battles are to be fought; let us fight them bravely." No luxuries for him. His headquarters often offered scarcely more comforts or better food than the tent of the private soldier; and when he ordered the army to march "light," he set the example by reducing his own baggage to the smallest amount possible. He slept under a shelter-tent, or bivouacked with his men with the sky for a canopy. At Shiloh, after the first day's battle, when he had personally given his orders for the attack the next morning, he lay down on the ground, with a stump for a pillow, and without shelter from the storm which raged, slept till the dawn called him again to unremitting labor. And he took good care of his men. He was always watchful over the quartermaster's and commissary departments, and wherever he commanded supplies came promptly to hand. During the period that he commanded the army of the Tennessee it never was short of food; and the only time when there was danger of such a condition, he promptly ascertained to what extent the rebel country would support his forces, and was one of the first to learn that important policy in the conduct of the war. He protected his men, too, from the imposition and excessive charges of sutlers by strict orders properly enforced; and when a steamboat captain, on the Mississippi, demanded an exorbitant sum for the passage of sick and wounded soldiers on their way home on furlough, he compelled him to refund the excess over a reasonable sum, at the risk of having his boat confiscated. "I will teach these fellows," said he, "that the men who have perilled their lives to open the Mississippi for their benefit cannot be imposed upon with impunity."

A commander so true to his men, and at the same time so able and successful as a general, could not but inspire them with respect, love, and confidence. He made no attempt to render himself popular, and never resorted to any clap-trap or pretence; but in everything he did for his soldiers, as in everything he did for his country, he was in downright earnest, and they knew it. For this they will always love him, as for the victories to which he led them they will always honor him.

## CHAPTER X.

After the War. — Generous to repentant Rebels. — Tour through the South. — Andrew Johnson's Usurpations. — Encouragement to the Rebels. — Grant's Measures to control the rebellious Spirit. — The New Orleans Riot. — Grant and Sheridan. — President Johnson's Tour. — Grant's Company ordered. — His Reticence and Escape. — Not to be caught again. — Confidence of Congress. — The military Districts and Commanders. — Execution of the Reconstruction Acts. — Grant's Firmness and Support of the Authority of Congress. — Johnson's Anger. — The General's Duties faithfully performed. — He anticipates Trouble. — Intrusted with extraordinary Power. — Johnson's Hostility. — Removal of Stanton. — Grant's Protest. — Johnson's Obstinacy. — Grant Secretary of War *ad interim*. — His rare administrative Powers. — Removal of Sheridan. — Another Protest. — Removal of Sickles and Pope. — Grant the Defender of Congressional Policy. — Johnson's "little Game." — He misrepresents Grant. — Grant's Letter to the President. — Johnson's vulgar Hatred. — He maintains his Version. — Grant's Reply. — The People's Judgment. — Failure of the "little Game." — Consequences to Johnson. — Contrast between Grant and Johnson.

THE return of peace imposed new duties upon General Grant, not, perhaps, so much to his taste as active employment in the field, but none the less faithfully performed. His headquarters were at Washington, where some of the citizens of the North, in gratitude for his great service to the country, presented to him a spacious and well-furnished house, with an excellent library well supplied with military works, and adapted to the use of the commander of the armies.

These and other free gifts from a grateful people were acknowledged with the quiet modesty characteristic of the man.

He who had done so much to crush the rebellion, who knew the terrible cost of the war in blood and treasure, who had learned by experience the spirit of the rebels, like all true and patriotic soldiers did not wish to see all that blood and treasure wasted, and all the toils, burdens, and sufferings of those four long years borne in vain. If the rebels, humbled and penitent, would accept in good faith the results of their foolish and wicked contest, and seek to restore the Union upon a permanent basis of freedom and justice, he was disposed to treat them leniently. It was in the hope of securing such a disposition on the part of the rebels that he had granted magnanimous terms to Lee's army, and by that precedent to all the rebels in arms. When, not long after the war, he made a tour of inspection at the South, he was encouraged by the conduct of most of those with whom he came in contact to believe that the great majority of the late rebels did honestly accept the situation, and were ready to submit to such conditions as the government might impose, in order to resume their relations with the Union, and restore the exhausted resources of their states. Such, undoubtedly, at that time was the sentiment of these men, so utterly defeated in the field, ruined in property, and hopeless, except in the clemency of their conquerors.

But Andrew Johnson, usurping the prerogatives of Congress, undertook to restore the rebel states according to what he denominated "my policy," and destroyed the fair prospect of a just settlement of the important questions involved in reconstruction. Without authority he appointed provisional governors, authorized conventions to frame constitutions, dictated who should vote, and on what conditions the states might be restored to the Union. And all this he did to secure to *rebels* and not to loyal men the power of reconstruction. He had declared that rebels "must take back seats," but he now pardoned them, and even appointed them provisional governors. He had promised to be the Moses of the colored race, but now all his efforts were directed to leading them back into virtual bondage. And that was the sum and substance of "my policy" — to restore all political power to the old slave-holding aristocrats who had risen in wicked rebellion, and to subject the colored race, who had been made freemen by the war and by amendment to the constitution, to a state of dependence and tutelage in no way better than slavery itself.

Encouraged by favors they had no right to expect, the old spirit of the rebels was soon made manifest. They no longer accepted their condition as conquered enemies of the republic, but arrogantly demanded the rights of citizens. They showed their hatred of Union men, and sought to oppress the freedmen as they had oppressed their slaves, bringing on again a state little better than war in some portions of the South, and exciting a spirit no better than rebellion.

General Grant had occasion to issue orders for the suppression of this rebellious spirit which grew out of Andrew Johnson's *policy*, and he became convinced that he had been deceived by the apparent humility of the rebels, or that the malignant spirit of the rebellion had become newly aroused by the action of the President, and could be controlled only by military authority. So far as the disposition of troops permitted, he gave orders for the protection of loyal white men and freedmen, and for the punishment of the atrocities of unrepentant rebels. His influence and his action, as might be expected, were all on the side of law and order, and against the arrogant and vindictive spirit which exulted in cruelty and atrocity.

Andrew Johnson's policy, and his direct communications with the Louisiana rebels, encouraged them to the most bitter opposition to the loyal element in that state, and caused the New Orleans riot of August, 1866, when they wantonly attacked the members of the State Convention, which had previously framed a constitution, and reassembled according to the terms of its adjournment. Whether the assembly was by proper authority or not, there was no justification for the bloody opposition manifested by the rebels, with Mayor Monroe and some of the state officials at their head. But the support and encouragement which they received from the President led them to commit the outrages and murders by which loyal men, white and black, were assailed, hunted down, and killed. General Sheridan, who commanded the department, and who was absent at the time in Texas, was not disposed to tolerate the rule of that rebellious spirit which he had fought for four years to conquer. He investigated the affair, and reported the atrocious spirit and acts of the rebels, and acting under the instructions of General Grant, he took measures for the protection of loyal men, and watched the schemes of these still malignant rebels. He was sustained and strengthened by Grant, although the rebels appealed to the President, and received all the aid and comfort he dared to give them. Sheridan's firm and loyal conduct gave great satisfaction to the people of the North, except to those who were ready to join hands with the rebels against Congress. But it was due to Grant's firmness and fidelity to the principles which had triumphed over rebellion, that the army was not at New Orleans and elsewhere at the South actually ranged on the side of the rebels against loyal men.

Soon after the New Orleans riot the President made his notable and notorious tour to the tomb of Douglas; and in order to create as much popular enthusiasm as possible, he invited, in the form of a command, General Grant and Admiral Farragut to join the presidential party. His course on that journey, "swinging round the circle," and making vulgar, undignified, and seditious speeches, must have disgusted these two patriotic veterans. Their presence served to bring out vast crowds, whose cheers the President was conceited enough to imagine were tributes to himself. But on more than one occasion it was made evident that the crowd came to cheer Grant and Farragut, and not Johnson, — the heroes who had conquered the rebels, and not the renegade who sought to restore them to power. Grant modestly acknowledged the honors offered him, but made no speeches, knowing that silence, after Johnson's tirades, was more eloquent and becoming than words.

Notwithstanding Secretary Seward's repeated insinuations that Grant supported and approved Johnson's policy, and his declaration that "General Grant cannot be separated from the President," the general improved the first favorable opportunity to leave the party. He had no taste for "shows;" he was indignant that he should be used to give *éclat* to the President's political tour, and be placed in a false light before the country; and he was disgusted with that functionary's vulgar manners and malignant speeches. He determined that he would no longer be subject to the imputation of opposing Congress and the will of the loyal people, and that he would not again be caught in such unworthy company. While the President, the next year, was on his tour to Boston, Grant returned to Washington from a visit to West Point. On the cars he met some ladies, who remarked upon his not being one of the President's party. "I was not invited," said the general, dryly, "and had I been, I should not have accepted the invitation."

When Congress assumed the prerogative which belonged to it, and prescribed the terms and conditions on which the rebel states might be restored to their relations with the Union; when it saw the necessity of affording protection to the freedmen against the oppression and outrages of their late masters and rebel opponents of emancipation, it was found necessary to use the military power to secure the desired results. Andrew Johnson had vetoed the "civil rights bill," designed to protect the freedmen; he had denounced, opposed, and almost undertaken to veto the fourteenth article of Amendments to the Constitution, which was designed as a basis of restoration of the states, and he had so indicated his hostility to Congress and to its policy, which was the policy of the people who had carried through the war, that it was necessary to provide for some executive power as far as possible free from the interference of his wrong-headed will. General Grant had given such evidence of his adherence to the policy on which the war had been carried through, and of his obedience to law, that Congress saw in him, as the head of the army, the officer whose authority and influence would aid in the execution of its laws, and oppose a barrier to the schemes by which the President sought to restore the rebels to power.

The rebel states were divided into five military districts, each to be commanded by a major-general. These officers were selected by Grant, though appointed to those places by the President, and in making the selection he took those whom he knew to be faithful to the policy on which the rebellion had been suppressed, and opposed to the restoration of rebels to power. Schofield, Sickles, Thomas, Ord, and Sheridan were the officers appointed to the several districts; but Thomas, desiring to remain in command in Kentucky and Tennessee, Pope was designated in his place. The authority of these commanders was great, but their acts were subject to the approval or disapproval of General Grant, who thus had the responsibility of the execution of the laws and the exercise of military power in the rebel states, so far as such responsibility could be separated from the President. It was necessary that this should be done in order to remove "impediments" to reconstruction, and to restrain the greatest of all impediments, Andrew Johnson, from thwarting the will of the people as expressed in the just measures of Congress. The result proved that the confidence of Congress and the people was not misplaced.

That the reconstruction acts were executed with any degree of fidelity and success, was due chiefly to General Grant. From him emanated the general instructions under which the military commanders acted, and with him rested the power to revoke or approve their acts. Like their superior, the commanders who were first designated for the several districts were faithful to the principles upon which they had fought through the war. They were obedient to the law, and knowing the spirit of those who opposed it, they were watchful and energetic in the performance of their duties. Had they been under the discretionary orders of the President, and consented to be the instruments of his will, no principle of reconstruction determined upon by Congress would have been carried out. Mr. Johnson's influence was constantly exerted against congressional reconstruction in every way in which he could make it felt; and his well-known bitter hostility to negro suffrage, his avowed hatred of the "radical" Congress, and his language and promise in his frequent conversations with the unsubmissive rebels who went to Washington to misrepresent the condition of southern affairs, and to secure his aid to their plans for thwarting the will of Congress, did more than anything else to prevent an early settlement, and rendered the duties of the military commanders more arduous.

But for the firmness of Grant, the influence of the President, and his rebel and Democratic supporters, might have been more disastrous. The general was determined to carry out the provisions of the law, so far as it was intrusted to the military authorities, whether it clashed with the purposes of Andrew Johnson and the rebels or not; and his subordinates, equally obedient to the law, and inspired and sustained by him, acted promptly and fearlessly. This conduct of Grant, and the military commanders, excited the anger of Johnson, who has always *hated* those who opposed his will and his opinions. Their removal of rebel civil officers, in governments which were merely tolerated till new and permanent governments could be established, were especially objectionable to him. Their full recognition of the rights of negroes, as secured by the reconstruction acts, was unpardonable. That they could act independently of him, and in opposition to his "policy," was intolerable. Their popularity with the people of the North, not only for their faithful service in reconstruction, but for their brilliant victories and brave deeds during the war, was an additional annoyance, for he did not dare to do what he most desired, and remove them all at once to make way for his tools, if he could find any.

Regardless, however, of Mr. Johnson's ill temper, Grant quietly performed his duties under the laws of Congress, and as commander of the army manifesting the same subordination to legitimate authority, and the same steady support of the policy of the loyal North, which he had shown during the war. He made no public declarations of his views, and did not undertake to construe the laws to suit any theory of his own, but executed them according to their plain intent and purpose. As a soldier, he abstained from a frequent expression of his political opinions, and his constitutional reticence made him appear still more cautious in that respect. But in private, among his friends, he did not hesitate to avow his sentiments, and those who knew him best were assured of his sympathy with the prevailing sentiment of the North, while his official acts satisfied even the most exacting. He won the entire confidence of Congress as an officer faithful in the administration of law as he had been able in his conduct of the war, and they saw in him the firm supporter of the laws, a barrier against the usurpations and schemes of the Executive to oppose and nullify the will of the people, as expressed by their representatives.

The bad temper, threatening language, and unscrupulous conduct of Andrew Johnson, foreboded trouble in some shape as soon as Congress adjourned, and the danger of impeachment, which was then first agitated, should not be imminent. So satisfied was Grant that the President intended to defeat the will of Congress in its reconstruction policy, if not even to do something worse, that he urged members of Congress not to adjourn without provision for reassembling in case of an emergency. Congress, though it made a partial provision of this kind, relied chiefly upon the passage of laws to restrain the President. The reconstruction act was amended in spite of a veto, and the tenure of office act was passed, designed, among other things, to prevent the removal of Mr. Stanton, who alone, in the cabinet, supported the congressional policy. Another act provided that the general of the army should always have his headquarters at Washington, that he should not be ordered elsewhere, nor be removed, except with the consent of the Senate, while all military orders were to be issued through his headquarters.

That Grant should thus be intrusted with extraordinary powers for the safety of the republic, as well as for the reconstruction of the rebel states, shows how strong was the faith of Congress in his integrity and fidelity to law and principle. The confidence of Congress was fully shared by the people, among whom he was regarded as the man for the next President,—a designation which made him doubly obnoxious to Johnson. Grant was too strong in the popular estimation, as well as in his position by law, for Mr. Johnson openly to quarrel with him, or to seek to remove him, however much he desired to do so. But bitter in his hostility to Congress, and to the faithful agents of its will, the President determined to do all he could to prevent the success of the congressional policy, and indirectly to assail or damage Grant. His purpose, soon made manifest, was to remove or suspend Secretary Stanton, whom he hated, and to put Grant in his place *ad interim*, and then to remove those military commanders at the South who were the most efficient in their execution of the reconstruction laws, and who were most highly esteemed and heartily approved by the general. In this way Mr. Johnson, while carrying out his policy of obstruction, hoped also to place General Grant in a false position, as the instrument of these removals, and to shake, if not destroy, the confidence of Congress and the people in him. To snub the general, by removing those who had obeyed his instructions, was another pleasant intention of this high-minded President.

But General Grant, though always subordinate as an officer, could not see such open disregard of the law, and such hostility to the will of the law-making power, without a protest, and when the purpose was announced to him, he addressed to the President the following letter, which shows his respect for law, his fidelity to principle, and his honest independence.

HEADQUARTERS ARMIES OF THE UNITED STATES,
WASHINGTON, D. C., August 1, 1867.

SIR: I take the liberty of addressing you privately on the subject of the conversation we had this morning, feeling, as I do, the great danger to the welfare of the country should you carry out the designs then expressed.

First. On the subject of the displacement of the Secretary of War. His removal cannot be effected against his will without the consent of the Senate. It is but a short time since the United States Senate was in session, and why not then have asked for his removal if it was desired? It certainly was the intention of the legislative branch of government to place cabinet ministers beyond the power of executive removal, and it is pretty well understood that, so far as cabinet ministers are affected by the "tenure of office bill," it was intended specially to protect the Secretary of War, whom the country felt great confidence in. The meaning of the law may be explained away by an astute lawyer, but common sense, and the views of the loyal people, will give to it the effect intended by its framers.

On the subject of the removal of the very able commander of the fifth military district, let me ask you to consider the effect it would have upon the public. He is universally and deservedly beloved by the people who sustained this government through its trials, and feared by those who would still be enemies of the government. It fell to the lot of but few men to do as much against an armed enemy as General Sheridan did during the rebellion, and it is within the scope of the ability of but few in this or any other country to do what he has. His civil administration has given equal satisfaction. He has had difficulties to contend with which no other district commander has encountered. Almost if not quite from the day he was appointed district commander to the present time, the press has given out that he was to be removed; that the administration was dissatisfied with him, &c. This has emboldened the opponents to the laws of Congress within his command to oppose him in every way in their power, and has rendered necessary measures which otherwise may never have been necessary. In conclusion, allow me to say, as a friend desiring peace and quiet, the welfare of the whole country north and south, that it is in my opinion more than the loyal people of this country (I mean those who supported the government during the great rebellion) will quietly submit to, to see the very men of all others whom they have expressed confidence in removed.

I would not have taken the liberty of addressing the Executive of the United States thus but for the conversation on the subject alluded to in this letter, and from a sense of duty, feeling that I know I am right in this matter.

With great respect, your obedient servant,

U. S. GRANT, *General.*

HIS EXCELLENCY A. JOHNSON,
*President of the United States.*

But neither reason nor the patriotic appeal of the foremost soldier of the country could prevail against the obstinate ill will of the President, and on the 12th of August he issued an order suspending Secretary

Stanton, and appointing General Grant Secretary of War *ad interim*. The general and the secretary were on the best of terms, and were agreed in their support of the congressional policy of reconstruction. While Mr. Stanton protested against the action of the President, there was no one to whom he would more readily yield the place than to Grant. And the general, who cordially expressed his "appreciation of the zeal, patriotism, firmness, and ability" with which Mr. Stanton had ever discharged the duties of Secretary of War, accepted the position in order that the department might still be administered in the interests of loyalty and the enforcement of the laws, and not be made the instrument of Andrew Johnson in opposing Congress and encouraging rebels.

Whatever might have been the motive of Mr. Johnson in appointing Grant, the people knew enough of that functionary to believe that it was not an honest desire to promote the welfare of the country. But it had an effect which was probably not intended, as it had a result which was not anticipated. If at first any doubts arose as to Grant's fidelity to the principles which he had hitherto supported, they were dispelled as soon as the facts connected with his appointment were known; and any fears for his capacity for civil office were also as speedily and certainly removed. The administration of the war department with regard to reconstruction was not changed, and its affairs were conducted with an energy, ability, and spirit of economy, which proved *that General Grant's rare administrative and executive talent was none the less suited to the discharge of civil duties than to the conduct of military affairs*.

General Grant had been but five days the acting Secretary of War, when Johnson commenced the other part of his programme, by issuing an order for the removal of General Sheridan from the command of the fifth military district, and for the assignment of General Thomas to that position. Being asked if he had any suggestions to make concerning this assignment, General Grant again protested against the movement as follows: —

HEADQUARTERS ARMIES OF THE UNITED STATES,
WASHINGTON, D. C., August 17, 1867.

. . . . . . .

I am pleased to avail myself of this invitation to urge, earnestly urge, urge in the name of a patriotic people, who have sacrificed hundreds of thousands of loyal lives and thousands of millions of treasure to preserve the integrity and union of this country, that this order be not insisted on. It is unmistakably the expressed wish of the country that General Sheridan should not be removed from his present command.

This is a republic, where the will of the people is the law of the land. I beg that their voice may be heard.

General Sheridan has performed his civil duties faithfully and intelligently. His removal will only be regarded as an effort to defeat the laws of Congress. It will be interpreted by the unreconstructed element in the South, those who did all they could to break up this government by arms, and now wish to be the only element consulted as to the method of restoring order, as a triumph. It will embolden them to renewed opposition to the will of the loyal masses, believing that they have the Executive with them.

The services of General Thomas in battling for the Union entitle him to some consideration. He has repeatedly entered his protest against being assigned to either of the five military districts, and especially to being assigned to relieve General Sheridan.

There are military reasons, pecuniary reasons, and, above all, patriotic reasons, why this should not be insisted upon.

I beg to refer to a letter marked "private" which I wrote to the President, when first consulted on the subject of the change in the War Department. It bears upon the subject of this removal, and I had hoped would have prevented it.

I have the honor to be, with great respect,

Your obedient servant,

U. S. GRANT, *General U. S. A.*,
*Secretary of War ad interim.*

HIS EXCELLENCY A. JOHNSON,
*President of the United States.*

The President, however, persisted in his encouragement to the unreformed rebels by removing General Sheridan, and as General Thomas's health would not justify his being sent to New Orleans, General Hancock was appointed in his place. On the same day General Sickles was removed, because he, like Sheridan, carried out the reconstruction acts in the interest of loyalty, and General Canby was ordered to succeed him. And subsequently, for similar reasons, General Pope was removed, and General Meade assigned as his successor. In making these changes, except so far as his petty ill will was gratified, Mr. Johnson must have been disappointed. For all the new commanders, except Hancock, honestly and faithfully administered the reconstruction laws in accordance with their plain intent and meaning, and with the general instructions of

Grant; and though Hancock was in some way demoralized, and became, perhaps unwittingly, the tool of the President in fostering the rebel element in New Orleans, most of his retrograde and unjustifiable orders were promptly revoked by Grant, not a little to the President's annoyance.

In all this, and in many other less apparent ways, General Grant has been the defender and enforcer of the congressional policy of reconstruction, which is the policy of the people who fought through the war and put down the rebellion. Faithful to the principles for which the North with so many sacrifices contended, and faithful to the memory of the thousands who laid down their lives for the suppression of the rebellion and its infamous spirit, he could neither be bullied, nor coaxed, nor deceived into a policy which should restore rebels to power and place loyal men under their heel. He has been, too, a barrier to the possible schemes of folly and madness which Andrew Johnson is said to have contemplated. His very presence at Washington, as commander of the army, has been the safety of the republic, and a constant intimidation to rebels, and to any executive usurpation in the interest of rebels.

When the regular session of Congress commenced in December, 1867, and Mr. Johnson, complying in one respect with a law which he assumed to declare unconstitutional and void, sent to the Senate his reasons for suspending Secretary Stanton, his "little game" was made apparent. The Senate refused its consent to the removal of Mr. Stanton, and, according to the intent of the law, he was immediately reinstated. General Grant, now as always obedient to the law, recognized the action of the Senate as itself a reinstatement of the secretary, and notifying the President of the fact, vacated the office. Mr. Johnson, baffled and angry, made known through some of his favorite correspondents of the press, his own schemes to thwart the will of Congress, in which he made it appear that General Grant had been a willing and active participant, but had finally been guilty of falsehood and deception, and had allowed Mr. Stanton to resume the war office in violation of his express promises. The substance of the statement was, in brief, that General Grant had promised the President that he would either hold on to the office of Secretary of War and resist the reinstatement of Mr. Stanton by the Senate, or, if he should change his mind and prefer not to be a party to the controversy, would resign, and thus enable the President to appoint some one who would be his tool; that on the Saturday previous to Stanton's reinstatement Grant virtually repeated this promise, and also promised to see the President on the following Monday, but failed to do so; and that at a cabinet meeting, being asked if he had not made such promises and broken them, he admitted that he had! The newspaper account, of course, did not fail to color the picture to Grant's disadvantage.

This story was published to gratify the vulgar hatred of Mr. Johnson, and with the hope of alarming the Republican party, and so damaging the general's reputation that the people would not accept him as a candidate for the Presidency. It was intended also to divert attention from Mr. Johnson's own guilty purposes. So mean a game was never before played by an occupant of the White House, nor indeed by any politician of respectability and position. But it did not succeed. General Grant, whose conduct through all his career had been straightforward, honest, and obedient to law, could not in decency submit to the imputations authorized by a President of the United States, although he was a man in whom, notwithstanding his high office, the country had learned to put little confidence. He addressed to the President the following letter, which palpably states the truth: —

HEADQUARTERS ARMY OF THE UNITED STATES,
WASHINGTON, D. C., January 28, 1868.

SIR: On the 24th instant, I requested you to give me in writing the instructions which you had previously given me verbally, not to obey any order from Hon. E. M. Stanton, Secretary of War, unless I knew that it came from yourself. To this written request I received a message that has left doubt in my mind of your intentions. To prevent any possible misunderstanding, therefore, I renew the request that you will give me written instructions, and, till they are received, will suspend action on your verbal ones.

I am compelled to ask these instructions in writing, in consequence of the many and gross misrepresentations, affecting my personal honor, circulated through the press for the last fortnight, purporting to come from the President, of conversations which occurred either with the President privately in his office, or in cabinet meeting. What is written admits of no misunderstanding.

In view of the misrepresentations referred to, it will be well to state the facts in the case.

Some time after I assumed the duties of Secretary of War *ad interim*, the President asked me my views as to the course Mr. Stanton would have to pursue, in case the Senate should not concur in his suspension, to obtain possession of his office. My reply was, in substance, that Mr. Stanton would have to appeal to the courts to reinstate him, illustrating my position by citing the ground I had taken in the case of the Baltimore police commissioners.

In that case I did not doubt the technical right of Governor Swann to remove the old commissioners and to appoint their successors. As the old commissioners refused to give up, however, I contended that no resource was left but to appeal to the courts.

Finding that the President was desirous of keeping Mr. Stanton out of office, whether sustained in the suspension or not, I stated that I had not looked particularly into the tenure of office bill, but that what I had stated was a general principle, and if I should change my mind in this particular case, I would inform him of the fact.

Subsequently, on reading the tenure of office bill closely, I found that I could not, without violation of the law, refuse to vacate the office of Secretary of War the moment Mr. Stanton was reinstated by the Senate, even though the President should order me to retain it, which he never did.

Taking this view of the subject, and learning on Saturday, the 11th instant, that the Senate had taken up the subject of Mr. Stanton's suspension, after some conversation with Lieutenant General Sherman and some members of my staff, in which I stated that the law left me no discretion as to my action, should Mr. Stanton be reinstated, and that I intended to inform the President, I went to the President for the sole purpose of making this decision known, and did so make it known.

In doing this I fulfilled the promise made in our last preceding conversation on the subject.

The President, however, instead of accepting my

view of the requirements of the tenure of office bill, contended that he had suspended Mr. Stanton under the authority given by the constitution, and that the same authority did not preclude him from reporting, as an act of courtesy, his reasons for the suspension to the Senate. That, having appointed me under the authority given by the constitution, and not under any act of Congress, I could not be governed by the act. I stated that the law was binding on me, constitutional or not, until set aside by the proper tribunal. An hour or more was consumed, each reiterating his views on this subject, until, getting late, the President said he would see me again.

I did not agree to call again on Monday, nor at any other definite time, nor was I sent for by the President until the following Tuesday.

From the 11th to the cabinet meeting on the 14th instant, a doubt never entered my mind about the President's fully understanding my position, namely, that if the Senate refused to concur in the suspension of Mr. Stanton, my powers as Secretary of War *ad interim* would cease, and Mr. Stanton's right to resume at once the functions of his office would under the law be indisputable, and I acted accordingly. With Mr. Stanton I had no communication, direct nor indirect, on the subject of his reinstatement, during his suspension.

I knew it had been recommended to the President to send in the name of Governor Cox, of Ohio, for Secretary of War, and thus save all embarrassment — a proposition that I sincerely hoped he would entertain favorably; General Sherman seeing the President at my particular request to urge this, on the 13th instant.

On Tuesday (the day Mr. Stanton reëntered the office of the Secretary of War) General Comstock, who had carried my official letter announcing that, with Mr. Stanton's reinstatement by the Senate, I had ceased to be Secretary of War *ad interim*, and who saw the President open and read the communication, brought back to me from the President a message that he wanted to see me that day at the cabinet meeting, after I had made known the fact that I was no longer Secretary of War *ad interim*.

At this meeting, after opening it as though I were a member of the cabinet, when reminded of the notification already given him that I was no longer Secretary of War *ad interim*, the President gave a version of the conversations alluded to already. In this statement it was asserted that in both conversations I had agreed to hold on to the office of Secretary of War until displaced by the courts, or resign, so as to place the President where he would have been had I never accepted the office. After hearing the President through, I stated our conversations substantially as given in this letter. I will add that my conversation before the cabinet embraced other matter not pertinent here, and is therefore left out.

I in nowise admitted the correctness of the President's statement of our conversations, though, to soften the evident contradiction my statement gave, I said (alluding to our first conversation on the subject) the President might have understood me the way he said, namely, that I had promised to resign if I did not resist the reinstatement. I made no such promise.

I have the honor to be, very respectfully,

Your obedient servant,

U. S. GRANT, *General.*

HIS EXCELLENCY A. JOHNSON,

*President of the United States.*

Mr. Johnson replied, repeating what he had before published through newspapers hostile to Grant and Congress, and adding that four members of the cabinet concurred in the general accuracy of the published statement. This called out the following manly and honest response from General Grant: —

HEADQUARTERS ARMY OF THE UNITED STATES,
WASHINGTON, D. C., February 3, 1868.

SIR: I have the honor to acknowledge the receipt of your communication of the 31st ultimo, in answer to mine of the 28th ultimo. After a careful reading and comparison of it with the article in the National Intelligencer of the 15th ultimo, and the article over the initials J. B. S., in the New York World of the 27th ultimo, purporting to be based upon your statement and that of the members of your cabinet therein named, I find it to be but a reiteration, only somewhat more in detail, of the "many and gross misrepresentations" contained in these articles, and which my statement of the facts set forth in my letter of the 28th ultimo was intended to correct; and I here reassert the correctness of my statements in that letter, anything in yours in reply to it to the contrary notwithstanding.

I confess my surprise that the cabinet officers referred to should so greatly misapprehend the facts in the matter of admissions alleged to have been made by me at the cabinet meeting of the 14th ultimo as to suffer their names to be made the basis of the charges in the newspaper article referred to, or agree in the accuracy, as you affirm they do, of your account of what occurred at that meeting.

You know that we parted on Saturday, the 11th ultimo, without any promise on my part, either express or implied, to the effect that I would hold on to the office of Secretary of War *ad interim* against the action of the Senate, or, declining to do so myself, would surrender it to you before such action was had, or that I would see you again at any fixed time on the subject.

The performance of the promises alleged by you to have been made by me would have involved a resistance to law, and an inconsistency with the whole history of my connection with the suspension of Mr. Stanton.

From our conversations, and my written protest of August 1, 1867, against the removal of Mr. Stanton, you must have known that my greatest objection to his removal or suspension was the fear that some one would be appointed in his stead who would, by opposition to the laws relating to the restoration of the Southern States to their proper relations to the government, embarrass the army in the performance of duties especially imposed upon it by these laws; and it was to prevent such an appointment that I accepted the office of Secretary of War *ad interim*, and not for the purpose of enabling you to get rid of Mr. Stanton by my withholding it from him in opposition to law, or not doing so myself, surrendering it to one who would, as the statement and assumptions in your communication plainly indicate was sought. And it was to avoid this same danger, as well as to relieve you from the personal embarrassment in which Mr. Stanton's reinstatement would place you, that I urged the appointment of Governor Cox, believing that it would be agreeable to you and also to Mr. Stanton — satisfied, as I was, that it was the good of the country, and not the office, the latter desired.

On the 15th ultimo, in presence of General Sherman, I stated to you that I thought Mr. Stanton would resign, but did not say that I would advise him to do so. On the 18th I did agree with General Sherman to go and advise him to that course, and on the 19th I had an interview alone with Mr. Stanton, which led me to the conclusion that any advice to him of the kind would be useless, and I so informed General Sherman.

Before I consented to advise Mr. Stanton to resign, I understood from him, in a conversation on the subject immediately after his reinstatement, that it was his opinion that the act of Congress, entitled "An act temporarily to supply vacancies in the executive departments in certain cases," approved February 20, 1863, was repealed by subsequent legislation, which materially influenced my action. Previous to this time I had had no doubt that the law of 1863 was still in force, and notwithstanding my action, a fuller examination of the law leaves a question in my mind whether it is or is not repealed. This being the case, I could not now advise his resignation, lest the same danger I apprehended on his first removal might follow.

The course you would have it understood I agreed to pursue was in violation of law, and without orders from you; while the course I did pursue, and which I never doubted you fully understood, was in accordance with law, and not in disobedience of any orders of my superior.

And now, Mr. President, when my honor as a soldier and integrity as a man have been so violently assailed, pardon me for saying that I can but regard this whole matter, from the beginning to the end, as an attempt to involve me in the resistance of law, for which you hesitated to assume the responsibility in orders, and thus to destroy my character before the country. I am in a measure confirmed in this conclusion by your recent orders directing me to disobey orders from the Secretary of War, — my superior and your subordinate, — without having countermanded his authority to issue the orders I am to disobey.

With the assurance, Mr. President, that nothing less than a vindication of my personal honor and character could have induced this correspondence on my part,

I have the honor to be, very respectfully,

Your obedient servant,

U. S. GRANT, *General.*

HIS EXCELLENCY A. JOHNSON,

*President of the United States.*

The President reiterated his version of the affair, with the further charge against Grant of insubordination; and he undertook to substantiate his statements by the certificates of five members of the cabinet. But it is significant, that of these indorsers of presidential veracity, those who are of the least political consequence, and the most obsequious followers of Mr. Johnson, give the briefest and most emphatic certificates of his correctness; while those who chose to exercise their own memory, though they do not contradict the President, whom they felt compelled to sustain, really show that General Grant's statement was the true one. Certainly every unprejudiced reader could not but believe the plain, straightforward, soldierly declarations of General Grant, which accord with his well-known character and acts, rather than the disingenuous statements of Andrew Johnson, who was bent upon disobeying law, and defying Congress, and was trying to force a loyal officer to share his guilt.

When the correspondence was placed before the people, they speedily rendered a verdict in favor of the tried and honest soldier. They saw that his fidelity to the country in time of peace, against the wily schemes of an unscrupulous executive, was as firm and true as it had been in war when contending against the armed forces of the rebellion. And Mr. Johnson had the satisfaction of seeing his little game of damaging Grant's reputation no more successful than his malignant and unlawful attempt to get rid of Stanton; for the general was only the more firmly fixed in the regards of the people, and all the more trusted by Congress. On the other hand, the unexpected result of Mr. Johnson's schemes soon followed this correspondence; for, continuing in his folly and madness, he boldly defied the law, and was impeached for high crimes and misdemeanors.

The contrast presented by Grant to Johnson is just what the country now needs in its chief executive in order to secure peace, stability, the legitimate fruits of a costly victory, and the sure return of prosperity. While Johnson, for his scandalous degradation of his high office, wrong-headed defiance of law, opposition to the will of the loyal people, and political apostasy, will be consigned to obscurity or infamy, Grant will be honored for his modest dignity, strict obedience to law, respect for the people, and fidelity to principle.

## CHAPTER XI.

Grant's Character. — His intellectual Ability proved. — Insight into the Character of others. — Wise Selection of Agents. — Tenacity of Purpose. — Firmness. — Obedience to Law. — Respect for the Will of the People. — Qualifications for high Positions. — Generosity to his Subordinates. — Reticence. — An inquisitive Visitor alarmed. — Judicious Silence at Washington. — No Speech-maker. — The Advantage of his Reticence. — Not repulsive or inaccessible. — Republican Simplicity. — No Taste for Display or Etiquette. — Two Weaknesses: Smoking, and driving Horses. — An Inveterate Smoker. — A Yankee Habit. — Horses and Fast Driving. — A false Accusation. — An Invention of Enemies. — His Features and Appearance. — Conclusion.

THE leading traits of General Grant's character have been indicated in the foregoing sketch of his career, but it may be well to group together some of the characteristics and habits which go to make up the man who now holds so prominent a position before the American people.

His intellectual ability, which early in the war was not appreciated nor even admitted among those who measured such ability by scholarship or brilliant success in some civil pursuit, has been fully proved. It only required the opportunities of war to develop itself, so that it should tower above his modesty, his undemonstrative manner, and retiring habits. After his successful campaigns, planned and executed with so much of skill and persistency; after Vicksburg, and

Chattanooga, and Richmond; after the skilful direction of movements on the most extended field of war which ever came under the supervision of one man, his intellectual ability cannot be questioned. Though not of a type to be called into exercise under ordinary circumstances, or rather being accompanied by traits of character which prevented its being called into exercise except under extraordinary pressure, it has proved itself in the most difficult field, and on the most important of occasions; and it has proved itself to be of that quality and character that it can be safely trusted to conduct prudently and successfully the affairs of a great country in time of peace as well as in time of war.

His remarkable insight into the character and capacity of others has been illustrated by his wise choice of subordinates to carry out his plans. It has been said that he owed his success to his able subordinates, and this idea has been encouraged by his own modesty and generosity towards them; but, in truth, they were more indebted to him than he to them. It was his sagacity which recognized their merit, and, in more than one instance, called them from obscurity, and gave them the opportunity of distinguishing themselves. It was his discernment which selected each to take that command, and to perform those deeds, for which he was best adapted. His most brilliant subordinates, Sherman and Sheridan, were especially thus indebted to him. Sherman was looked upon as little better than a lunatic till Grant gave direction to his abilities, and Sheridan achieved no distinction till Grant, seeing his true capacity, made him his cavalry commander, and sent him to the Shenandoah to defeat Early, and to Five Forks to break through Lee's lines. Thomas, McPherson, and others, were in like manner indebted to Grant for promotion and opportunities; and each of them was trusted and assigned to difficult duties, because of his intuitive knowledge of their ability and fitness for the work demanded of them. So, also, his staff has always been composed of men admirably qualified for their respective duties, and who performed them with the same quiet energy which characterized their chief. This power to discern the character and ability of others, and to make a wise selection of agents, is one of the essential traits of a genius for command and for administration; and it is one as important for complete success in civil affairs as in military. Should General Grant be called to the higher position to which the people wish to promote him, the country has reason to feel assured that his wise choice of counsellors and executive officers will secure the most honest, faithful, and successful administration that has been vouchsafed to the country for many years.

His tenacity of purpose is another trait which has been illustrated through his whole career, and which is so prominent in the foregoing narrative of each of his campaigns, that it is needless to do more than allude to it here. Happily, in Grant persistency is united with patriotism, honesty of purpose, and sound judgment, which give it direction and exalt its character.

Allied to this is his firmness, which, being entirely free from conceit, never degenerates into obstinacy, although Mrs. Grant says "Mr. Grant is a very obstinate man." His firmness is generally for a good purpose, and subordinate to reason. He does not adhere to an opinion simply because he has expressed it, but only when he is convinced it is right; and when he has adopted a course which he is satisfied is the true one, he is not to be turned aside by opposition or flattery. Self-reliant and independent, by nature and by long training, he is not easily moved by the various advice of various men, but he calmly listens, weighs, and acts upon his own conclusions. He can say "no" to unworthy office-seekers, and keep political schemers at a distance, as he did the cotton speculators, who sought to bribe him when he commanded on the Mississippi.

But with all his firmness and independence, he has always manifested the strictest obedience to law, and submission to legitimate authority. This was illustrated throughout his career during the war, and it has been especially shown in his efforts to carry out the provisions of the reconstruction acts, against the adverse influence of Andrew Johnson, the sneers and opposition of northern Democrats, and the schemes of perverse rebels. Again, in his respect for the tenure of office act, he resisted the machinations of the President and his advisers to disregard the law, and involve him in a violation of it. His obedience to law has always been based upon respect for the source of law,—the will of the people. He conducted the war in accordance with the declared policy of the loyal people, and in his protest against the removal of Stanton and Sheridan, he boldly told Mr. Johnson, "It is more than the loyal people of this country (I mean those who supported the government during the great rebellion) will quietly submit to, to see the very men, of all others, whom they have expressed confidence in, removed;" and again, he reminded him, "*This is a republic, where the will of the people is the law of the land. I beg that their voice may be heard.*" Thus, by his acts and by his language, he has put himself upon record, and established his reputation as a true democrat, and a thorough republican, whom the people can safely trust.

Such traits of character, possessed in a remarkable degree by General Grant, admirably qualify him, not only for the high position, and the important command and trusts to which he has been called, but for the still higher functions for which the loyal people have everywhere designated him. But besides these, he possesses other traits becoming that high position, if not so important to it, which commend themselves to the admiration of the people, and to their love.

He has always manifested a noble generosity to his subordinates, — a generosity which has won their firmest friendship, and the genuine respect of his soldiers. No one more heartily rejoiced in the successes of his brother officers than he; no one more warmly commended them for their gallantry and good service; no one more earnestly supported them in the hour of danger and trial. No petty jealousy ever disturbed his relations with any officer in the army; and if there were some whose capacity he doubted, or whose conduct he censured, it was never because of any mean prejudice, ungenerous rivalry, or narrow ill will. Never acting from impulse, his judgment of others was always founded on reason, while a kindly nature has made his favorable judgments all the more friendly and his unfavorable opinions less harsh.

Much has been said about General Grant's reticence, and it might be supposed from some accounts that he is mute as a statue. But, on the contrary, though he is not loquacious or demonstrative, and never seeks opportunities to express his opinions, he is often very agreeable in conversation, and is straightforward, honest, and simple in his language as he is in all his conduct. But upon all matters connected with his official action he is discreetly reticent. During the war he never announced his plans or talked about them, except with those whom he could absolutely trust, and his staff officers, following his instruction and example, were equally silent.

When he took the field with the army of the Potomac, he was frequently beset by members of Congress, correspondents of the press, and visitors favored with special passes to the front, who endeavored to elicit from him something of his views and purposes. But they were always unsuccessful, and were obliged to be content with the most general remarks, from which they drew inferences to suit themselves, or were put off with quiet monosyllables, which sometimes alarmed their fears and sometimes wounded their conceit. Impertinent querists and officious advisers often retired from his headquarters utterly baffled in their purposes, and uncertain whether to be angry or not. A characteristic anecdote of such an interview is told.

A visitor to the army, during the brief quiet which followed the battle of Spottsylvania, called at the general's headquarters, and found him talking with one of his staff, and smoking as usual. The stranger, who had studied strategy to his own satisfaction, encouraged by the absence of all ceremony at headquarters, ventured to address the commander, and inquired, —

"General, if you flank Lee, and get between him and Richmond, will you not uncover Washington, and leave it a prey to the enemy?"

"I reckon so," replied the general, indifferently, discharging a cloud of smoke, perhaps to conceal a quiet smile.

The visitor, encouraged, again asked, "Do you not think Lee can detach a sufficient force from his army to reënforce Beauregard, and overwhelm Butler?"

"Not a doubt of it," replied Grant, promptly.

The stranger, finding that his views were so readily accepted by Grant, asked again, "Is there not danger, general, that Johnston may come up from Carolina and reënforce Lee, so that with overwhelming numbers he can swing round and cut off your communications and seize your supplies?"

"Very likely," coolly replied the general, knocking the ashes from his cigar. The stranger, alarmed at all these dangers admitted by the general, and amazed at his indifference and stolidity, hurried away to startle the timid with a vivid account of the critical position of affairs.

Such was Grant's reticence while conducting the war, and the country saw abundant reason for applauding it. After the war, when he established his headquarters at Washington, where he was continually surrounded by impertinent inquirers and political schemers, that reticence was none the less needed, and was as discreetly practised. If they endeavored to entrap him, they were completely foiled by quiet monosyllables or a blunt change of the topic. If schemers talked politics to elicit his views, he could "talk horse," as a subject with which he declared himself more familiar; and it is related that when President Johnson undertook to find out what he thought of the rumored intention of the Democrats to nominate him for the presidency in order to flank the Republicans, he replied, "I think — this is the poorest cigar I ever smoked."

As for making speeches, he is utterly averse to doing so; and on many occasions when the people, aroused to enthusiasm by his presence, have called him out, he has in the briefest possible manner thanked them, and excused himself, or called upon some friend to respond for him. There is no danger of his making speeches, under any circumstances, which would compromise himself; but in view of the speech-making of Mr. Johnson, Grant's silence is a virtue more precious than gold.

By his discreet reticence, General Grant has avoided many embarrassments which a more loquacious and demonstrative man might have experienced in the atmosphere of Washington; and, in avoiding embarrassments, he has also saved the country from the excitement and alarm which the ever-changing rumors of his sayings and opinions might produce. But if he knows when to be silent, he knows also when and where, and to whom, he can talk frankly and without reserve. And his views and opinions thus expressed harmonize fully, and always, with the conduct and acts which have proved his devotion to the country. He is, in words as well as deeds, a firm, unhesitating supporter of Congress in its reconstruction policy, and a strenuous opponent of executive usurpation and disregard of law.

Though retiring and undemonstrative in manner, he is by no means repulsive or inaccessible. On the contrary, he is easily approached, and is courteous and pleasant. But the citadel of his thoughts and purposes he does not yield either to the bold assaults of brazen inquisitors, or to the wary approaches of cunning diplomatists.

Of all the distinguished officers in the army, Grant has always been the most unostentatious and unpretending in appearance and manner. He is careless, but not slovenly in his dress, and is so devoid of any air of importance, that but for the four stars upon his shoulder-straps, no one would suppose he was more than a hard-worked quartermaster's subordinate. In the winter of 1865, shortly before his final and triumphant campaign, while in Washington, he visited the Capitol, and was received with becoming respect by the members of Congress. But so quiet and modest was his deportment, that when he retired from the Senate chamber, a Democratic senator declared that "a gross mistake had been made in appointing Grant lieutenant general, for, in his opinion, there was not a second lieutenant of the home guard of his state who did not 'cut a bigger swell' than this man who had just left their presence!" Such is his modesty and simplicity of demeanor on all occasions, except when at the very front he gives orders on the field of battle; and then his energy and determination assert themselves above his modesty and usual quiet.

During the war there was no parade about his headquarters, which was no more pretending in appearance or arrangement than a colonel's, while his "headquarters train" was often the smallest in the army. In the winter of 1864–5 he lived in a small log-house on the banks of the James, sleeping on a common camp cot, and eating with his staff at a table furnished with such simple food as "roast beef, pork and beans, 'hard tack,' and coffee." No body-guard ever accompanied him simply for display, and he never made a show of good-looking, well-dressed, and formal orderlies about his headquarters.

The same simplicity he continues in his position as general of the army, at Washington. While not wholly negligent of the proprieties of life and of his office, he discards all useless display, and seems to deprecate all unnecessary formalities. No punctilious etiquette is necessary in order to reach him; and no omission of customary form would call down his wrath on the head of any careless or ignorant offender, though some brigadier generals have in that way manifested their importance. In truth, his whole style and bearing afford an example of *republican simplicity* remarkable in a successful military commander, but not inconsistent with true dignity, nor unbecoming in the high office he now holds, or the higher office which awaits him.

But General Grant is human. Though possessing a genius for command in war, and sterling qualities which fit him for high executive duties, and inspire the confidence of the people, he is not an immaculate hero. He has two weaknesses: he loves to smoke a good cigar, and he loves to drive good horses. There are some persons to whom even these weaknesses, in a man like Grant, commend themselves more than rigid virtues; and there are few who, while they appreciate his high qualities and well-balanced character, will like him any the less for such tokens of a genial humanity.

He is an inveterate smoker. He smokes on almost all occasions when there is not an absolute impropriety in the indulgence. And sometimes the force of habit has been so strong that it was necessary to remind him of the propriety of laying aside his cigar; as once, when he visited the Capitol, and was about to enter the Senate chamber as the most distinguished guest of the Senate. So on more than one occasion the guard over ammunition wagons has been obliged to repeat to him the orders, "No smoking allowed here, sir!" Like a gentleman and a soldier he always good-naturedly complied with such suggestions, whether there is danger of a social explosion or an explosion of gunpowder.

Smoking, with Grant, acts as a sedative rather than as a stimulant. During the war, in the most trying times of anxiety, while awaiting the result of movements vital to success, and in the most exciting moments of battle, he smoked incessantly, and, to all outward appearances, as calmly as if his mind were not burdened with the heavy responsibilities and duties of his position and the time. He smoked while laying his plans and consulting his officers in his tent, and while, on the battle-field, he watched the eventful contest and gave his orders for skilful manœuvres or for the decisive charge.

With smoking he sometimes combined the Yankee habit of "whittling" when deep in thought or anxiously awaiting results; and in the Wilderness is a tree which he industriously hacked with his penknife while the great battle raged, as if smoking alone were not enough to keep the outward man quiet while his mind was occupied with the great events around him, and the great purposes within. So, in front of Vicksburg he smoked and whittled while watching the mounting of some guns in an important position, utterly regardless of the bullets of the enemy's sharp-shooters which whistled about him.

As for his love for driving good horses, it is what might be expected of one whose earliest trait was a love for, and command over, a horse. That trait was developed so early in his boyhood, that it must have been born in him, and is not the result of education or association. He knows a good horse, and knows how to drive one; and he has too much humanity to abuse the animal he loves. He is said to be one of the best riders in the army, as might be expected from his early habit of riding, though his physique does not render him the most showy. In these times of peace, he prefers to ride in his carriage and drive. If once or twice he has driven a little faster than the snail-pace gait which municipal laws allow, he was simply up with the times; and when some vigilant policeman, prompted by fun or malice, complained of him for violating an ordinance against fast-driving, with his usual deference for law, he modestly acknowledged his error, and promptly paid his fine.

It has been alleged that he has a more serious weakness, which would be less pardonable in the eyes of the people. At various times during the war, malignant enemies charged that he was grossly intemperate in his habits; and since he became, by his acts, identified with the party which seeks to reap the just fruits of victory over a wicked rebellion, Copperhead presses have asserted, or meanly insinuated, the same charge. No allusion would be made here to such accusations but for the gross injustice which has been done him, in thus seeking to create a prejudice against him in the minds of a large number of people. It is sufficient to say, that those who know him best, who have been most intimately associated with him during the war and since, pronounce such charges utterly false; and that gentlemen, earnest in the cause of temperance, have satisfied themselves that there is no foundation for the assertions and insinuations derogatory to his character in this respect, but that he is a man whose temperance cannot justly be called in question. Such charges originated in personal or political enmity, and have been encouraged and circulated through total misapprehension of Grant's temperament and manner. They are the mean and malicious inventions of those who, during the war, hated him for his victories; those who have always sympathized with the rebels whom he conquered, or those who have supported the policy of the man who publicly disgraced the country when he became Vice-President. Narrow prejudice and ignorance, which are ever ready to misapprehend, have given credit and circulation to the libel; but it is none the less a libel, unsupported by any evidence worthy of belief.

The photographer and engraver have made Grant's features familiar to the public as first among the heroes of the war. Those features indicate the modest and reticent character of the man, as well as that persistency and firmness which are among his most prominent traits. Quiet and retiring in his appearance, there is yet an air of reserved power in his look and manner which his career has abundantly proved that he possesses. He is of medium height, rather under than over the average standard, and has a very slight stoop of the shoulders.. With all his retiring and modest expression, and absence of pretension of every sort, there is in his manner a quiet dignity, and a courteous but unceremonious bearing, becoming his position. He has, too, a pleasant smile; and at times a keen glance in his gray eyes tells how closely he observes. He can give a cordial greeting to a guest; but his very look seems to read the motives of men, and inform him when to close his heart and his thoughts against sycophants and selfish schemers. While honest merit will meet with a quiet welcome, place-hunters and corruptionists will find little encouragement in his face or in his words.

General Grant has not infrequently been compared with him who holds the first place in the reverence of the American people. Though it is not proposed here to trace the resemblance between the two,—an attempt which would be distasteful to no one more than to our modest general,—it may with truth be said, that, more than any other one man the "saviour of his country" on the battle-fields of the recent unparalleled rebellion, Grant deserves to have a stronger hold upon his countrymen than any man since Washington. Contending for principles no less noble, and in a cause as just, he achieved victory on a grander scale; and, possessing many of the traits of the illustrious "Father of his country," he may well receive, at the hands of a people saved from anarchy and ruin, the highest rewards they can bestow, and be called to preside over a Union dedicated to Liberty, Equality, and Justice.

As by his victories he has proved himself "first in war," so by his patriotism, ability, fidelity to principle, moderation and firmness in civil life, he may yet be hailed as "first in peace," and still be, as he now is, "FIRST IN THE HEARTS OF HIS COUNTRYMEN."

www.ingramcontent.com/pod-product-compliance
Lightning Source LLC
LaVergne TN
LVHW011231110826
845150LV00006B/1603

* 9 7 8 1 4 2 5 5 1 4 5 4 9 *